STYLE YOUR HOME

DESIGN SECRETS FOR STYLING WITH CONFIDENCE

EMMA BLOMFIELD

Hardie Grant

BOOKS

To my friends whose homes became the grounds
and inspiration for this book.

And to Shirley and Markie, who both taught me
so much about the meaning of home.

INTRODUCTION

I have spent many years working as an interior designer making other people's homes more functional, practical, beautiful and elegant. I've had no formal training. I've learnt everything I know on the job, working for other uber-talented designers, learning from my clever colleagues and peers, and renovating my own properties.

Clients engage our services when they've got difficult layouts or design challenges that have them stumped. Each time we wrap a project as a team, we sit down and assess what worked and what didn't work so we can better our skills and services as a business. I realised after a while that these experiences were also helping to shape the concept of this book.

I noticed clients, friends and family members kept asking me a lot of the same questions, especially around placement and dimensions. This book tells you how to do the styling and designing. It shows you *exactly* where to place items and how to lay out your furniture. It gives you every dimension detail so you can confidently go and order curtains that fit your windows and pendant lights that sit perfectly above your kitchen table, and more.

Our homes are ever evolving. They are a constant work of art that changes just like our lives. This book is for anyone who is interested in the world of decorating and renovating, or keen to learn while embarking on their own home remodelling or new build. Wherever you are in the process, it should help provide you with the answers you have been searching for.

My aim was to collate the struggles of renovators and decode the interiors industry, which many people find bewildering. My hope is that you'll use this book as your style guide and handbook to help ease the stress of a renovation, or to make furniture shopping before moving into a new home easier.

Our job as decorators and designers is to create stylish spaces that are highly practical and functional while looking good. That's no mean feat. Trying to delicately balance practicality with beauty is difficult. I still struggle to achieve this balance so I never judge when clients, friends or family members come to me and my team and say they feel defeated by the design process and need some help.

Designers go with their gut in so much of what they create for clients. I run on instinct every single time. I'll be walking through a project or sitting at my computer designing a room and saying, 'I'm just not feeling it!' Then I'll stumble on the perfect tile, paint shade or door knob and suddenly it'll kick off the rest of the project with ease because it now 'feels' right. How can you learn this skill? This book shows you specific styling skills you can implement yourself without second guessing your decisions because it is all laid out for you to put into action.

All of this takes time and there's no point in aiming for total perfection because that day will never come. So embrace the mess and chaos because laughter and fun usually accompany both of those things and that's where really wonderful memories are formed. At the end of the day, what all interior designers are selling is a feeling. We help you buy furniture and nice possessions to create a lovely feeling when you open the doors to your home. And that feeling is priceless.

Our homes should include the character of each person who lives there. This is where we create strong memories of our childhood through parties, sibling memories (good and bad!), home-cooked meals and generational gatherings.

We all love boundaries and directions in life. So this book explores my tried and tested formulas to help guide you in the right direction with styling and renovating all those corners of your home that you haven't yet been able to get right. It's important to use your imagination too, because when you can successfully inject some of your own personality into a home it really becomes a reflection of your true self.

We talk a lot about our homes being a reflection of ourselves and others who live there, but why do we place so much importance on this? It's rooted in a number of psychological factors that are deeply ingrained in our need for self-expression, comfort, identity and also belonging. Our values are shaped so heavily around our home life.

Writing this book and living through my own renovations helped cement what I value.

- A safe haven to unwind in after work.

- Entertaining family and friends. I've always loved having people in my home and being able to cook for them and share memories.

- Quality appliances to cook with because I enjoy cooking and baking.

- Spaces to style and display meaningful trinkets from my travels or gifts from loved ones.

- Bespoke finishes that are unique to me. This one is really important. I want something very different from what I usually create so it's a clear reflection of my own style and personality, separate from what I create for others.

- Quality bed linen. If we spend more than a third of our lives sleeping, it makes sense to me from a cost per use perspective to be as comfortable as possible.

I often think about our attachment to a space. When you think about it, it's actually quite odd to be so attached to something that can't love us back. Yet our homes are *so* much more than four walls. They're where we form strong emotional bonds, feel safe and secure, shape our identities, accumulate history and create a sense of belonging.

Decorating and styling

DECORATING IS LIKE STORYTELLING, BUT FOR YOUR HOME.

GETTING STARTED

You've probably picked up this book because there's something bothering you about the look or feel of your home, or perhaps you're wanting to further educate yourself on what makes a house a home. Decorating and styling your home don't just beautify your space, they allow for creative expression and improve functionality. This, in turn, will have a positive impact on your well-being and enhance your quality of life, as well as the people you live with and those you entertain. So it's important to educate yourself and be aware of practical choices you can make to decorate and style your home for your own enjoyment.

So let's dive in and explore exactly how you can embrace the art of decorating and styling.

Consider the architecture

It is important to take the architecture of your home into consideration, so that you can make careful selection of furniture and design elements to preserve or do justice to its history. This can also help alleviate the many decisions required in the planning process, as you'll have clear design options from the era when the home was built. For example, there are so many design elements specific to the 1920s, such as fluting, fans, geometrics, terrazzo, brass and rich jewel tones, which instantly narrow down your design choices very quickly. Your trades or design team can also help you with these design elements, no one more so than an interior designer who has studied these eras in detail and who would have worked on many homes from varying periods.

If you're working with a brand new home then your choices are vast, which can be confronting and overwhelming when planning. Look at your geographic location, family structure, budget and personal style and taste, as well as how you live, work and play at home to help shape your brief for the design. Carefully following the steps in this book will help carve out a clearer path for you, free up some decision-making space and allow you to clearly articulate your vision for your home.

Have fun with the process and don't take it too seriously. These elements are to be used as a guide to help you inject your own fun and personality into your space. It's not a competition and no one is going to come in and mark your work after you've finished. Art and design are both very subjective topics so, while there are principles and elements you can follow, they are open to interpretation to allow you to creatively express yourself.

Think outside the square

There's always an opportunity for the unexpected in the world of design. That's what makes art so fascinating. Making mundane and boring items pretty and exciting adds a tiny bit of joy to your life and your home.

Think about when you stay in a hotel and you notice all the tiny design details, such as a decorative tissue-box cover, an attractive wastepaper bin or stylish soap dispenser. Each of those things has been carefully designed and crafted for no other purpose than to be pleasing to the eye. Think about what little details you can pay attention to in your home to make it a more beautiful space.

You don't have to buy everything new. Using items you already own tells a story about you and is meaningful or sparks conversation with guests.

Trends come and go

If you're buying items in retail stores then you're buying trend-based furniture. The furniture buyers spend their year sourcing furniture and homewares to fit the latest look, customer feedback, fashions and technology.

If you want to pursue a more timeless look, there are other choices you can make.

- Custom design and manufacture your own products for a unique and tailored look.

- Know that nothing is ever truly timeless. You'll end up needing to repair or replace things with time and use. What you choose now, regardless of trends, can only withstand so much use before it starts to show signs of wear and tear.

- Research products prior to purchasing. For example, marble is a timeless material but its uses in the home can be trend driven. A marble benchtop in the kitchen might not date but a marble-topped coffee table might within a few years.

What's a vignette? A grouping of personal objects or homewares that tell a story of the home's occupants by displaying them carefully on a flat surface in your home.

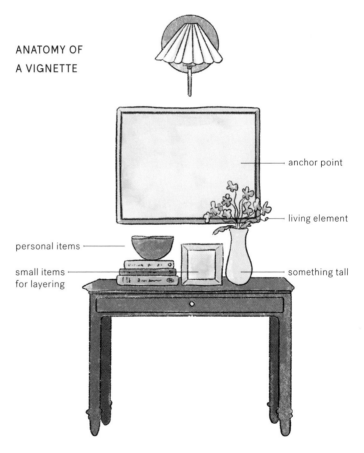

ANATOMY OF
A VIGNETTE

anchor point

living element

personal items

small items
for layering

something tall

Style Your Home

Preparing the space

Professionals in the home renovation industry don't jump into a client project without a significant amount of project research beforehand. You need to follow similar guidelines in order to avoid making dire mistakes.

Thankfully the prep work is relatively painless and if followed closely will save you time, money and loads of unnecessary arguments with the others who live with you.

CONCEPT MOOD BOARDS

Do you struggle to articulate your preferred interior design style? Sometimes it's actually easier to identify which styles you don't like first. This will narrow your options down.

It might also help to ask your friends, family or partner if they have any thoughts on your style. If they know you well enough they will have observed other homes you've lived in or bought you gifts and worked out what you do and don't like.

Mapping out a visual element is really important before you start choosing furniture, wall paint colours, floorboards and more. The mood board becomes your single reference point from start to finish on your home renovation or decorating project. Visuals help keep you aligned with your original vision for the house without you being steered into the wrong direction as things evolve. The renovation or new build process is a really long one and it's easy to lose focus along the way, so having a single document that helps keep you aligned with your goal is most important.

This little activity will help you with this process.

1 **SOURCE:** Rip out 20–30 images from magazines or save images that speak to you from places such as Pinterest or Instagram in a folder on your tablet or laptop . You don't need to make sense of it just yet. It's a research exercise to find rooms, furniture, colours and textures you like.

2 **REVISE:** Review all the images you've collected. Delete or cull any that no longer fit the project so you're only working with images that really resonate.

3 **ANALYSE** Grab a notepad and write down any common elements you notice in all your images. For example, are all the kitchens grey cabinets with brass handles? Or are all the sofas tan leather? Write these down as they will help form your style.

4 **CREATE:** Add all these images to a Pinterest board or print them off and make your own mood board with a corkboard. You should ensure that you're using images that show colour palettes, textures, textiles, detailed imagery of furniture, and close-ups of certain textures such as tiles or wallpapers.

This becomes your go-to document, which you should refer to throughout your project. If you're working with trades, show them this when you're walking them through your renovation plans. If you're working with a designer, this is probably the homework they'll ask you to prepare before you meet so that everyone is on the same page regarding the end result.

Remember, a picture paints a thousand words. Using imagery with everyone involved in the process will help illustrate your goal much more easily than if you try to explain your plans in words.

COMMON INTERIOR STYLES

HAMPTONS

HOTEL LUXE

MID CENTURY MODERN

FRENCH PROVINCIAL

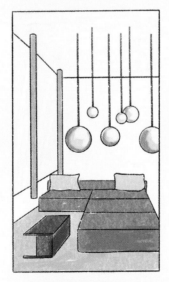

INDUSTRIAL

MODERN FARMHOUSE

PARISIENNE

HOLLYWOOD REGENCY

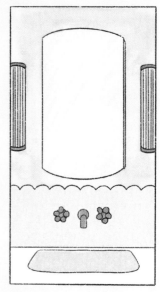

ART DECO

EARTHY ECLECTIC

MINIMALIST

JAPANDI

Style Your Home

1 Measure up

Knowing your dimensions well before commencing work on your project will help you significantly in the long run. Take note of all the little measurements because you'll be surprised how often you need to know the depth of your windowsill or the height of your ceiling.

Your trades/contractors will refer to all measurements in millimetres or inches. So if you are measuring anything for them make sure you indicate which system you are using to avoid confusion.

Document your measurements on your phone or in a project notebook. Having the details on your phone means that you can quickly refer to your notes when you're purchasing items for the house; for example, bathroom square meterage/footage for tiles or sink dimensions.

2 Plan your layout

The next task is to map out the layout of your rooms. This is a crucial step and often best outsourced to professionals. Designers, architects and builders or contractors can help you solve the trickiest of floor-plan layouts so, if in doubt, ask for help.

There are also many apps and software programs to help you create floor plans using the measurements you gathered in step one. This is discussed in detail on page 67.

3 Pick your palette

A preliminary look at colour schemes is helpful in the early stages of your planning. If you're not ready to commit to specific colours yet, thinking about undertones will help guide you in the right direction when you are ready to decide.

WARM UNDERTONES   COOL UNDERTONES

Undertones are generally warm or cool. Which you choose is completely up to you and your personal preference. However, warm tones are usually more appealing. They're softer, more inviting and welcoming, and flattering to the complexion. Cool tones are calming but can make a space feel cold and uninviting.

WARM UNDERTONES: Citrus tones such as yellows, oranges, browns, pinks, reds, taupes, creams, beiges and sandy colours

COOL UNDERTONES: Seaside colours such as blues, greens, teals, greys, crisp whites, lilac and purple

Whites can have both warm and cool undertones. Typically, a cool white is seen more in locations such as hospitals, dentists, office spaces, retail stores and other task-oriented spaces to allow for maximum light levels. Painting your home a cool white might make your room feel stark and harsh. Many modern, new builds opt for a crisp cool white to contrast against striking features such as polished concrete floors, stone tiles and steel features. Cool whites are also the most popular whites for exterior paint colours.

Warm whites are more commonly used in older homes as they complement more heritage colour palettes and warm timber tones, but that's not to say there isn't a place for them in modern homes. They add a lovely welcoming touch to a room as they more closely resemble natural light. Warm whites are excellent choices for lounge rooms, dining rooms, bedrooms and entry hallways.

And don't forget black. It's a great colour to chameleon between both undertones. You would think black was a cool undertone, but it works just as well in a warm-toned room as it does in a cool-toned room. So don't be afraid to include it in your colour palette.

Understanding the elements of styling

THE ROAD MAP NEEDED AHEAD
OF YOUR STYLING JOURNEY

TEXTURE

Textures have such an emotive component to them. Have you ever walked into a hotel room and thought 'Wow! I just want to jump onto that bed and get cosy'? Chances are it is because of layered textures – from bed linen to wallpaper to tiles to bedhead upholstery to flooring.

There are also smaller tactile moments you can enjoy in a room. It could be light switches you delight in toggling on and off or surfaces you stroke or keep wanting to touch when you walk by, such as a lovely wallpaper or upholstered dining chair.

Why do we like the tactility and why is it important to consider when layering a home? Tactility evokes memories and helps regulate feelings. For example, stroking a pet can help calm you down or relax you. How great is it walking into a homewares store and running your hands over blankets, throw rugs and bed linen, and imagining them in your home? There are so many different textures to consider – from smooth to shiny, rough to fluffy, rippled to bumpy and beyond.

Designers often use fabulous textures such as sheepskins, woollen rugs, cotton throw rugs, glazed pottery, jute rugs, leather sofas and velvet armchairs. There's something about those textures that cry out to be touched.

Textures have an incredible ability to enhance, and add depth and diversity to the look of a room, often without even adding colour. Beautiful tactile textures encourage you to engage with your surroundings by touching and feeling, which, in turn, helps you to connect on a deeper level with your environment.

So what kind of textures exist out there to help you build a story within your home?

Fabric

Fabrics work hard to add texture and tactility to a room. When you first think of textures you'll probably think about different types of fabrics such as linen, cotton, wool, velvet, gauze, silk and suede.

Where you use different fabrics greatly depends on the function of the room. Lightweight textiles such as linens and cottons that can billow in the breeze keep upholstery light and bright. Wool and velvet with their heavier weight evoke cosy vibes.

I always check how linen feels before buying it because I want to make sure that what I'm sleeping on feels really lovely and comfortable.

Fabrics work well layered together to give a more vibrant feel. Add dimension to your room by layering cushions, throws, curtains and rugs.

Don't forget about contrast. Fabrics can be emphasised easily when contrasted. For example, pair rough textures with silky smooth textures that make you want to sit down and touch them both.

Fabrics have a magical ability to create cohesion between rooms. This is often a difficult task for homeowners and renters to get right. So repetition of some of the same fabric textures (although not necessarily the colours) helps to tell a cohesive story as you walk through the house.

When choosing fabrics you will need to pay attention to a number of factors.

MARTINDALE RUB TEST: The natural wear and tear of a seat covered in fabric is rubbed against over and over to test its abrasion resistance.

MATERIALS: Do you want a natural or a synthetic material? Natural materials are more breathable, nicer to sleep on, sit on and touch. But they can warp and stretch a lot more easily than a synthetic material. Keep this in mind when choosing sofa fabrics or curtains, which could hang and drop over time.

USES: A fabric label on upholstery or drapery should always indicate whether it is intended as light domestic, general domestic or heavy duty commercial.

Wallpaper

Wallpapers can add a third dimension to your space with the use of geometric or even 3D shapes and elements. They can be a focal point or just a muted colour to add an additional texture layer for interest or cohesion with another texture in the room.

Unlike fabrics, wallpapers are generally used vertically in a space, so their colour and texture need to be assessed in a different way when applying it to your room. There are many benefits to using wallpaper. It can add drama with colour and texture, personality with fun shapes and themes, and mood and atmosphere. Your sensory experience can be enhanced, especially using wallpaper made from grass cloth, vinyl silks, linens and metallics.

USING WALLPAPER

- Create a feature wall either behind a sofa or a bed.

- Commit to the entire room, for example a powder room, and give your guests a fun surprise when they walk in.

- Use it sparingly for an added boost of texture as an accent; for example, in between wainscotting panels or behind bookshelves.

- Make a temporary update with removable wallpaper on a nursery or child's bedroom wall. When they outgrow the theme of the wallpaper you can peel it off with ease.

- Use wallpaper as a form of art by adding a big striking feature in the room.

- Depending on the texture and colour of the wallpaper, use it to blend in or stand out. Grass cloths in soft neutral palettes are a great way to add texture to the wall without detracting from other features in the room.

- Add a luxurious touch with textures such as silk or linen, especially those with a metallic sheen. Instant hotel luxe vibes!

Timbers

The beauty of using wood to add texture to a room is the added benefits of discovering and exploring the stunning timber grains, knots, swirls and imperfections in each piece of timber, leaving us in awe of what nature can create. Timbers used in juxtaposition with other elements in a room such as glass, steel, stone and metals create a dual enhancement.

Timber is perhaps one of the most versatile elements of all and there are very few areas that don't benefit from its texture. Whether it's on the floor or panelled up a wall, exposed ceiling beams, furniture or window surrounds – there really are a thousand and one uses for it in your home.

Think beyond naturally sourced hardwood timbers, too. There are loads of alternatives that will inject timber textures into your home and give you the benefit of their warmth.

TYPES OF TIMBER

ENGINEERED: Made from layers of solid wood, plywood and solid hardwood to create a highly durable floorboard, which is ideal for use in high-traffic areas or over concrete slabs. Engineered timbers come in a massive range of timber varieties and stains, making it an ideal choice for most residential homes.

HARDWOOD

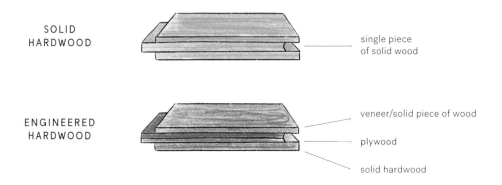

SOLID
HARDWOOD

single piece
of solid wood

ENGINEERED
HARDWOOD

veneer/solid piece of wood

plywood

solid hardwood

LAMINATE: A cost-effective way to introduce a wood-look timber floor without breaking the bank. Laminate flooring is thin-pressed wood layers of a repeating image of printed wood set onto a fibreboard or MDF core.

LAMINATE

LAMINATE

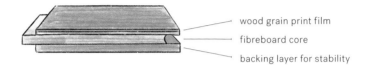

wood grain print film

fibreboard core

backing layer for stability

VINYL: Not a timber but is used to mimic timber floors and comes as a roll or individual tiles. Vinyl flooring can have a wood-look image printed on it that is highly durable and budget friendly. However, it does look like an obvious replica of timber, so is not an ideal choice for mid- to high-budget homes.

CORK: Although not typically thought of as a timber, cork is sourced from the bark of cork oak trees and mixed with resin to form a hard-wearing flooring option. Cork is generally used as tiles for flooring although it can be made in a roll.

Rugs

Rugs are a tactile texture for your feet to enjoy and can be easily layered with other rugs to create visual interest in a room. Layering a rough textured sisal rug with the softness of an antique Persian wool rug instantly lifts a room and elevates its look. A rug has the ability to zone and add cohesion by dictating the placement of furniture and carrying a repeated texture or colour palette through a room. Rugs are covered in much more detail on page 134.

Stone

Want to evoke a sense of bringing the outdoors in? The simplest way to do that is to incorporate some stone elements into your interiors. From benchtops to bathroom flooring to kitchen splashbacks, there are hundreds of applications for stone that enhance a room's textural elements. You might decide to use stone as a focal point and invest in beautiful natural stone slabs for your bathroom walls. Or perhaps you're concerned about budget, so an engineered stone is your preferred choice to revamp a tired kitchen benchtop.

One of the most beautiful benefits of using natural stone is not just its tactility but also its ability to change its appearance depending on the levels of natural light. The way the sun sparkles on natural stone is enchanting and inviting to touch.

Try to vary the application of stone to avoid an overload. Floors, walls, benchtops, fireplace surrounds, skirting boards, splashback or a striking feature wall are all great ways to incorporate stone textures. But if you use stone for all these features it will feel cold and uninviting.

COMMON TYPES OF STONE

TRAVERTINE: This natural limestone is usually in warm beige or grey tones.

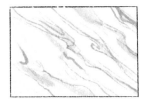

MARBLE: This natural stone has been used for centuries because of its durability and wide-ranging uses, from kitchen benchtops to floor tiles, fireplace hearths and mantels, sills and table tops.

GRANITE: This has a similar hardness to marble but is extremely resistant to scratches and difficult to stain. It is usually used for flooring and benchtops.

LIMESTONE: A sedimentary rock used as floor tiles, limestone is good for cladding and exterior pavers.

SLATE: Regaining popularity, slate is easily shaped into thin slabs, and is stain resistant and highly durable. It is used for flooring, hearths and benchtops.

SANDSTONE: This porous stone is made from quartz and silica and available in a range of beautiful neutral tones from warm brown to yellow. It is ideal for pool-edging tiles, courtyards, indoor flooring tiles, cladding and more.

CERAMIC AND PORCELAIN TILES: These are made from clay fired in a kiln to make a really dense and hard-wearing tile or benchtop.

ENGINEERED STONE: This is a great choice for budget-conscious homeowners wanting a natural stone look without the price tag. Engineered stone is made from a mix of quartz and resin and, unlike natural stone, is really resistant to spills and scratches.

Paint

Paint has the ability to make colours and textures recede or intensify depending on its placement. Typically, areas you want to recede should be painted in darker tones – in a similar way to the concept of wearing black in order to minimise lumps, bumps and bulges. So if you have a wall with imperfections or irregularities, try painting it black or a darker colour instead of white, which can unwittingly enhance imperfections because it allows so much light to bounce from the irregularities. This is effective for exposed ceilings in warehouse- or industrial-style homes where the services such as air-con vents, fire hoses and sprinkler systems are exposed. Spraying the ceiling black means much of that blends in and is far less obvious.

The same rules apply to making rooms appear larger or smaller. Sometimes it's best to lean into the lack of size by painting the room a deeper shade rather than trying to paint it white in the hope of making it feel larger. In some cases there's no tricking anyone into thinking a room is larger than it seems.

Think about these things when choosing paint to add a textural element to your home. Paint is obviously a relatively flat texture as it's a liquid that dries solid, but its application is what counts. Paint can also be distressed to give it a completely different texture if you're painting an antique piece of furniture and want it to have a more lived-in feeling.

PAINT TEXTURES

FLAT: Ideally used for ceilings, it draws the eye up and makes the walls appear as tall as possible.

MATT: Great to hide imperfections on your walls, but it can mark quite easily so use it sparingly on interior walls and ceilings.

LOW SHEEN: This is the most commonly used paint type for interior walls.

SEMI GLOSS: This is a great choice for skirting boards, window architraves and other trims.

GLOSS: This is a good option for a front door, especially with older heritage homes.

If you have picture rails, don't paint the walls a light colour underneath and a dark colour above the rail. Draw the eye up and elongate the room by continuing the light paint colour up the wall or switch to a half strength of the same colour.

Window treatments

Not just useful from a functional point of view, window treatments such as curtains and blinds help add lovely layers to your home and can create a cosier feel by lessening the harshness of a timber or aluminium window trim. Opting for a soft linen, floor-length sheer curtain transforms your room from a cold and harsh space to a warm and welcoming one almost instantly.

Curtains are such a tactile element that allow you to engage with the room when opening or closing the curtains. Texture is also added when sunlight hits the curtains or blinds, and creates shadows and patterns as the sun filters through.

Getting your fabric choices right for your curtains and blinds is important. Choosing something too heavy will influence how you feel in the room. Equally, going with something too light will have an impact on how the sun is filtered and the temperature controlled, as well as privacy.

Window treatment options are discussed in each chapter focusing on different rooms.

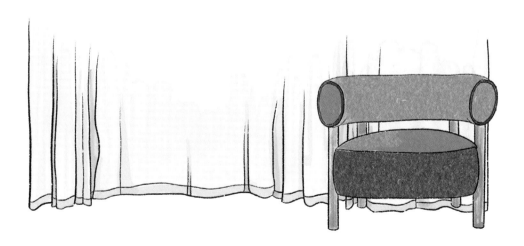

Metallics

The use of metallics adds a textural layer that exudes luxury. Door hardware, mirrored furniture, light fixtures and switches, tapware and more can add texture, interest and sophistication.

Mirrors are a great metallic element, and when hung opposite a light source such as a window or low-hanging pendant, they allow more light to bounce into the room. Mirror-topped furniture helps with this, too.

Metallics can either be the main feature of the room, such as a stunning gold chandelier hung above your dining table, or used as an accent to enhance smaller features such as brass door knobs on timber joinery. The application of metallics in your rooms is like adding jewellery to your outfit before you walk out the door – enhancing and beautifying.

Adding life

No room is ever really complete without the addition of something alive. Plants and flowers are obviously the easiest way to add life to a room. They bring a whole host of different textural elements with them, from spiky cacti in colourful pots to a beautiful sleek orchid for your dining table. They can either be a striking feature or blend into the background, such as a potted fiddle leaf fig tree in a corner.

Plants can be used to fill spaces that may be too small for a piece of furniture but don't quite look right blank and empty. They are great nook fillers and give vibrancy to a plain corner of the house.

FIDDLE LEAF FIG

RUBBER PLANT

SNAKE PLANT

CACTUS

MONSTERA

SUCCULENTS

TEXTURE

CONTRAST

Contrast is the second of the five elements of styling and highlights the difference between two or more elements, which contributes to a well-rounded room.

A room without contrast is boring and plain. When you add some contrast you suddenly find that the room is more exciting and intriguing. It can also help draw attention to something you want as a focal point. For example, you could paint the wall behind a really light and bright piece of artwork a very deep dark colour to help highlight the lightness of the art piece, rather than having it blend into a white or neutral wall.

Contrast allows you to highlight or add depth and dimension to a room. You end up with layers that can be peeled away so that more about the occupants of the house can be discovered. It can also help bring a sense of calm or tranquillity to a room by balancing textures on opposite ends of the spectrum.

Colour

People have such strong feelings about colour. Think about how picky you've been in the past about choosing the colour of your car, your hair, your jeans or the perfect coloured cushion. The list goes on …

Colour is such a powerful element that can evoke so many emotions and memories – some good, some bad. You will care deeply about choosing the right colours because not only do you want those colours to support everything else in the room, you also know how much it dictates the rest of the colours in the house. Every colour decision can be a paralysing choice. If you mess up the choice of paint colour for your walls, it affects the art you hang, the sofa you choose and the lighting you pick. There's a huge knock-on effect.

And then there's the indecision about choosing a neutral colour palette. Will that sandy beige tone work with the soft greige? It's a swift spiral into panic that can lead to a last-minute decision because the builders are asking you what colour you want for the walls. And the painters are coming the next day! If you're reading this and nodding your head in agreement, you're not alone. It's a battle homeowners universally face.

So how do you incorporate colour into your home? It actually comes down to following a formula to help you cheat your way to colour palette success.

COLOUR FORMULA

The colour wheel rule consists of three segments.

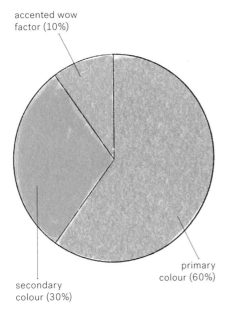

accented wow factor (10%)

secondary colour (30%)

primary colour (60%)

THE COLOUR WHEEL RULE

Still stuck? The same colour formula rules apply to putting an outfit together. Pants: 60 per cent; top: 30 per cent; shoes: 10 per cent.

PRIMARY COLOUR (60 PER CENT): Usually a neutral as it's the largest use of the colour. If you're feeling bold and love colour then this can be a big, bold, bright colour, too. This would be used for items such as your bed, sofa, dining table, wall-to-wall bookcase, kitchen cabinets, and bathroom tiles or benchtop.

SECONDARY COLOUR (30 PER CENT): A non-polarising colour such as blue or green, which works well with many other colours when put together in a room; for example, an armchair, side table, coffee table, bookshelf, rug, dining chair, or curtains and blinds.

ACCENTED WOW FACTOR (10 PER CENT): This is when you layer in your pops of colour such as a peachy pink or a lemony yellow. It will cover the least amount of surface area but be a nice little punch of colour to bring your colour palette together nicely. Accent pieces would be cushions on the bed or sofa, an artwork, flowers, ceiling colour, books or throw rugs.

COLOUR WHEEL RULE

When creating your colour scheme, think about all of those elements incorporated with high contrast or complementary colours to give the palette some interest.

Doing a neutral colour palette well is tough going. The key is texture. Make your room interesting by varying the textures you opt for. Sure, there are textures that will all be a neutral shade, but the fact that you may have a cream-based silky texture with a rough linen in a flax colour means that the rough and the smooth give the room more contrast and stop it looking flat and dull.

Pattern

Patterns, like colour, can be a polarising topic in interior design. Just like fashion, pattern trends come and go, probably even more so than colour trends. Many patterns are so closely associated with a certain era that it can mean they're completely ruled out by homeowners who associate a particular pattern with their grandparents' era, or have vivid memories of a particular quilt in their adolescence and never wish to relive those days!

Classic patterns that are timeless in their design such as stripes, toile, herringbone, florals, tartan, gingham and houndstooth are far more likely to be used in larger areas of the home to avoid dating.

If you're wanting to take more of a risk or modernise your interiors, some more contemporary patterns include geometrics, ikats, animal print, graphic prints, trellis, abstract and waves.

There are also plenty of instances when a more traditional pattern has been manipulated and morphed to become modern and contemporary. It all comes down to where you place it in the home.

You can create scale contrast by mixing the scale of the patterns, and style contrast by mixing pattern styles such as gingham, solid colour and so on.

Types of patterns to consider adding to your home:

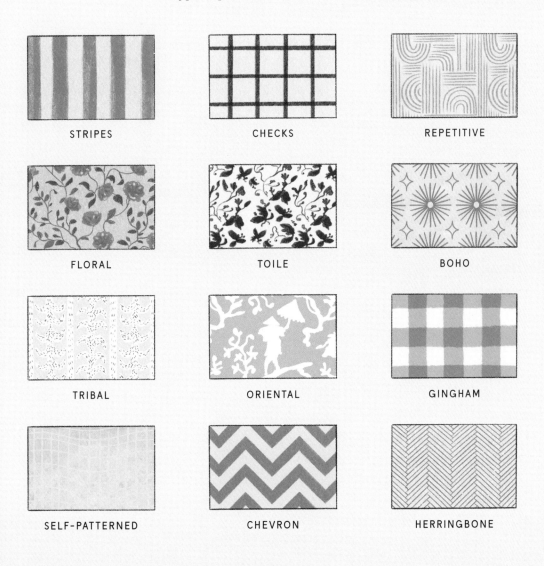

STRIPES

CHECKS

REPETITIVE

FLORAL

TOILE

BOHO

TRIBAL

ORIENTAL

GINGHAM

SELF-PATTERNED

CHEVRON

HERRINGBONE

Visual weight

When designers talk about visual weight, they're referring to mixing solid items with delicate ones for contrast rather than having too many of the same-sized items grouped together.

This approach can be applied to everything; for example, the size and shape of your sofa, armchair, dining table, chairs and sideboard, as well as bookshelves and coffee-table trays.

Solid items give your room or vignette an anchor point to work from and this means you can add to the vignette or room around that one solid feature. Skinny, fragile or delicate items get lost when grouped together because there's no solid weight to the pieces that your eye can rest on when looking at them as a whole.

Geometric or angular shapes are heavier items compared to more organic shapes that are lighter in visual weight, so think about incorporating both into your room or coffee table for contrast.

LAYERS

Create visual interest and depth by layering the different elements of styling. A beautifully layered room can feature a mix of sheers and blockout curtains, cushions and throw rugs, artworks and mirrors, bookshelves styled with books, as well as decor items such as boxes, photo frames and objet d'art.

HEIGHT

Height is yet another element to consider for a well-designed room. Most furniture generally sits at a maximum of 90 cm (35 in) from the floor up. If your room has a ceiling height of 280 cm (9 ft), then you've got a fair amount of open air between the top of your furniture and your ceiling. So how do you fill it?

 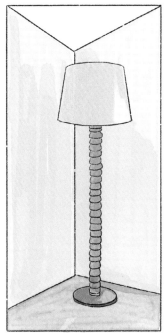 

Add bookshelves, tall plants or floor lamps for vertical contrast in a room with lower furniture. Curtains are also an excellent way of drawing the eye up.

If your budget allows, installing joinery from the floor to the ceiling is another excellent way to add height to a room as well as storage!

Hanging pendants from the ceiling is also effective and fills that gap between the ceiling and the furniture really well.

Art can fill the vertical space in a room, so choose an artwork that is well proportioned to the wall. A great designer trick for adding height is to choose an extra large artwork that fills an entire wall, which also gives a grand feel to the room.

And lastly, think about cascading tall to short items so there's less contrast between the two heights.

BALANCE

Just like all things in life, our homes need balance! Balance comes in a variety of forms and can be tricky to achieve. When done well, it means your room is visually pleasing, organised, nice to be in and comfortable.

If your home is feeling overwhelming or chaotic, chances are you haven't achieved true balance between form and function. A lack of storage is usually the biggest indicator that something isn't quite right because there's too much clutter. You find yourself tripping over things or you can't find something, and you feel stressed when you're meant to be relaxing.

Achieving balance is something you may find you need to work at regularly to keep the visual chaos quiet and under control. The following ideas should help bring some more balance to your home and create a functional yet aesthetically pleasing space for you to enjoy.

Symmetry

Symmetry, when done well, gives a sense of order and harmony which, in turn, gives a sense of luxury because it implies that a level of thought and effort went into collecting the items on the shelf, fireplace and sideboard. That attention to detail is similar to the level of care given to crafting luxury items such as custom-made upholstery or a couture gown.

Symmetry also has the power to give a sense of order. It is pleasing to the eye and easier to achieve because you're using two of everything. For example, two sides of the bed, two lamps, two cushions, two pillows, two European pillows and a pair of artworks above the bed.

A central focal point gives you a single focus for your vignette or room when there are no natural ones such as a window with a view or a fireplace. Symmetry also helps balance the weight of the room by having a central item to rest your eye on when looking at the vignette as a whole.

Decorating for the holidays? Use symmetry when styling your mantel for Christmas, Hanukkah, Halloween, Thanksgiving, birthdays and so on.

Use your camera to work out a good focal point. Seeing the space in 2D rather than 3D allows a different perspective.

Asymmetry

Asymmetry is the complete opposite of the previous element. While it sounds like a nice way of saying 'Anything goes!' and 'Do what you want and call it asymmetry', there are some basic principles to follow to avoid it looking like total chaos.

Achieving successfully placed asymmetrical items is harder than symmetry because it requires a level of irregularity that can look really messy and unstyled. Eastern cultures embrace asymmetry with design aesthetics such as feng shui, wabi-sabi and yin and yang, elements of which have been adopted in the western world.

Asymmetry is best accomplished using materials found in nature. There's so much beauty in the irregularity of naturally occurring elements, such as river pebbles, bird nests, feathers, shells and other found objects. Incorporate these with made materials that also embrace wonky or wild elements, such as rough-textured, handmade linen, hemp or jute rugs, brushstroke wallpapers and oil-on-canvas artworks by artists who practise wabi-sabi techniques.

Overlapping items rather than lining them up like little soldiers is a much more pleasing arrangement.

Imitating nature, which is known for its irregularity, is a beautiful way of expressing your personality and creative flair. It's engaging to look at and feels a bit less staged and more authentic than symmetrical placements. So if you're aiming for a really lived-in look, asymmetrical furniture placement and trinket styling is your friend. Not only does it provide a more relaxed and casual feel, it can also help highlight interesting elements in a room.

It also means you can mix and match different shaped and weighted objects, which can be more fluid and eye-catching with their lack of predictability.

PAIRS

Using pairs of things, such as cushions, candlesticks, curtains, armchairs, plants, artworks, lamps, bedsides, pendants over a dining table or kitchen island, or wall sconces in a hallway is an easy way to get balance.

Drawing the eye upwards with vertical lines, for example tongue and groove panelling on your walls, moulding down a hallway, tall cabinets, floor lamps, tall plants and floor-standing mirrors, makes your room appear taller.

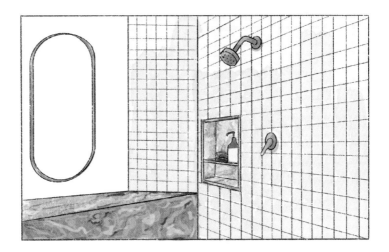

Repetition and cohesion

Feeling lazy? Repetition is the styling element for you.

Repeating elements throughout the house, for example using the same timber tone on the floor, fireplace mantel, floating shelves and artwork frames, adds to the cohesion of a room.

Creating a cohesive look throughout your home without repeating every element is really tricky. The best way to do this is to choose some small elements to repeat. For example, if you have a marble splashback in your kitchen, repeat that marble element on your fireplace mantel or bathroom benchtop to keep the textures and colours consistent.

A word of warning, however; you can overdo an element! If you're repeating finishes or materials throughout the house, where do you start and stop? Go back to your colour formula (60–30–10). If your main colour tone is being repeated, that's okay because you have 60 per cent to fill. But if it's an accented piece that you're repeating over and over, you'll tire of it faster and it will overwhelm the space.

If budget constraints restrict your ability to do the same elements throughout, what can you do instead to still get impact?

EXPENSIVE MATERIAL: Marble can be a costly material to work with, but if it's something you love and want throughout the house and you don't have the budget for it, use it more sparingly rather than overdoing its use in one area. For example, if you can't do a full marble fireplace, why not just do a marble mantel and timber for the remainder.

IMITATE: Using similar textures or colours, products such as engineered timber or stone is often a good way to imitate the real thing without the price tag. If you can afford to use real timber in certain areas, use a laminate or engineered wood in other areas to bring costs down.

SLIM DOWN: Another great hack is to use thinner profile benchtops than you have in the main kitchen in your butler's pantry. You're still repeating the stone look but you've saved yourself a few pennies.

Anchor points

Every room and every vignette needs an anchor point. It gives you a spot to focus on as it captures your attention when you first walk into a room, and then serves as the starting point for exploring the rest of the room with your eyes. If it's a room with lots of layers to it, you definitely need an anchor point because the layers can overwhelm you.

An anchor point gives stability to a room, defines different zones, provides cohesion to your space and helps set the tone for the room's style and design. It also allows you to enhance architectural features such as a fireplace, picture window, structural support and built-in joinery. It becomes the talking point for the room too, with each item holding a story that sparks a conversation, whether it is a piece of art you brought back from a family holiday in the Greek islands or a grandfather clock you inherited from your grandparents.

Groupings

You've got the choice between odd and even groupings. Odd groupings are more visually intriguing and allow for an organic look with a variation of size and quantities, whereas even groupings look a little too structured and predictable. Stylists and designers generally go for the odd option when arranging trinkets on their coffee tables as it looks more appealing and interesting.

Grouping things together allows for experimentation. Try grouping like with like (candlesticks, shells, etc.) or use a grid to divide the surface area of what you're styling or divide it into four. (Use triangles for round surfaces.)

The lounge room section (see page 89) shows you some helpful grid patterns and layouts to cheat your way to a beautifully styled grouping of objects on any of your flat surfaces.

Breathing space

This might be listed last but it's by no means an element to skip in the decorating and styling game. Allowing gaps and space around the items you're working with makes the room complete. You can be standing in a space that feels not quite right. Often it's because there's not enough breathing space between the styling elements so they feel too squashed.

A great tip designers use is to take a photo of the vignette you're styling or the area of the room you're struggling with. Seeing the space in 2D form allows you to see the flaws in greater detail and helps you work out what you need to tweak or change to make the room 'feel' right again. Sometimes moving a few items a couple of centimetres away from the next piece of furniture will be enough to give it more visual weight or presence in the room.

PERSONALITY

If you crave a space that feels like you, showcases your family's quirks, gives insight into the things you love most in life and makes you smile every time you walk in the front door, this element will help achieve all of those things.

People usually feel a strong pull to personalise their space shortly after moving into a new home. You will want to put your own stamp on a place that may have been renovated by someone else. This is not something people always excel at, and it can be a fine line between adding nods to your interests and experimenting a little too much.

By going through and personalising your home you immediately get a sense of ownership and control over your environment. It helps your children settle into a new home that they may not find familiar in any way and contributes to everyone's sense of belonging.

There are a number of ways to inject little snippets of personality into your home, and the good news is that a lot of them are free, cheap or what you already have lying around the house!

Found objects

Found objects doesn't mean things you've found on the street that others have left out for collection! Rather it refers to feathers, leaves, quills, stones, deserted nests, shells, driftwood and so on. All of these can be arranged in a shadow box or basket on your coffee table to remind you of a beach holiday or a farm stay.

Family memories

This is the ultimate way to show off some personality. Polaroids, mementos from holidays or even children's art from school up on the wall are inexpensive ways to remind you of beautiful memories and show others a bit more about who lives in your home.

Flowers

Adding flowers ticks off a number of elements of styling, adding colour, texture, fragrance and memories. They might be flowers you've picked from your garden (or Grandma's garden), a gift from a partner to commemorate an anniversary, or maybe a vibrant birthday bouquet from friends. Yes, flowers have an expiry date but they have this beautiful way of brightening up your home and making you smile every time you walk by.

Heirlooms

Heirlooms are some of the most magical objexts you can add to your home. They're often things you already have such as cutlery, crockery or vases. There's something so special about putting items on display that have been handed down to you. Maybe it's a serving dish your mother used every time you went over for a Sunday roast and now you use it to serve dinner to your own children. Or maybe it's something of almost no value that you played with on your grandmother's dressing table as a child and that now sits on your fireplace mantel piece and reminds you of happy times when you were young.

However, mixing old and new can be tricky, especially if it's an heirloom you've inherited that's quite large and striking and very obviously old world. Chances are, though, if you have a meaning attached to an item, you'll generally find a way to make it work. Refer back to the elements on previous pages for inspiration, such as repetition of colour, mixing up textures and grouping like with like.

Gifts

Loved ones who have spent time looking for beautiful trinkets or meaningful items for you to display in your home creates one of the most amazing love languages. Showcasing gorgeous gifts is another lovely way to inject character and charm into your home, with the added bonus of your friend or family member spotting their gift on display.

Cultural heritage

Family background plays a huge role in shaping our personalities, sense of belonging and identity, especially for children growing up and learning about their ancestors and family heritage. The most common way to incorporate cultural heritage into your home is through art, ceramics, textiles, and religious or spiritual items. Each piece you add that holds cultural significance helps add aesthetic value, and a source of pride and connection to your roots.

The other beautiful thing about incorporating cultural heritage is that it helps preserve traditions, customs and history, and keeps it alive for generations to come.

Personalised accessories

Nothing spells personality like a highly customised item, such as monogrammed coasters, napkins, mouse pads, notebooks and ring dishes. Or maybe you've commissioned a beautiful artwork from a local artist or saved up for years to have a special piece handcarved for your home. These personalised pieces are special to you and could become heirlooms for the next generation.

Collections

Nothing piques a guest's interest like a grouping of special collectables such as records, books, china, vases and antiques. These items tell a story and spark conversations that give insight into the personalities and characteristics of the people who live in the home.

Art

Where to even start with art! As the saying goes, beauty is in the eye of the beholder, and this couldn't be more true for artwork. What one person finds incredible, the next may find horrendous. But that's all part of the personalisation process and is the ultimate expression of your personality.

Art can do so much for a room. It adds colour, texture, scale, visual weight, interest and focal points. It can also help make small spaces feel larger than they are.

Art has the ability to trick the eye. You can fake a view for the room, making it feel like you're looking out a window to a beautiful vista, by hanging a large landscape painting or print featuring a bush or beach setting.

You can fill a blank wall with a gallery grouping of family photos to show who lives there, the family tree and beautiful family memories. If you don't want to hang an entire gallery of art on one wall, pairs work beautifully, too. Pairs usually come in portrait shape (vertical) or squares. Hanging two pieces together can be a great way to elongate a room. Vertical pieces stacked together draw your eye up and work better on skinny or narrow walls with plenty of height, such as up a staircase or at the end of a double height entryway.

Homemade items

Just like gifts and heirlooms, handmade pieces can be a really meaningful way to inject personality into your room. It can be children's preschool artwork, a tapestry from your grandmother to mark the birth of your first child, a vase you made in a pottery class or a DIY candle. There are so many different ways to use homemade items around your home.

Style Your Home

FUNCTIONALITY

The previous elements all focus on form and beauty, but a huge part of the design and decorating process is about practicality and functionality. If the room doesn't work for you and how you live because you've filled it with impractical yet gorgeous items, then you'll always find yourself frustrated.

Mapping out the functionality of a space before you move into it is the first step in the design process. It's not a sexy or exciting element but it serves you well in the long run if you spend time at the beginning of the process thinking about it.

You also need to consider flexibility and adaptability when it comes to functionality, as your needs are always changing and evolving. Families expand, pets are adopted, family dynamics shift or loved ones are lost.

A space that successfully blends functionality and beauty is one that allows for plenty of storage, is well organised, adaptable, comfortable, sustainable, considers longevity and supports your lifestyle.

Getting functionality right can often be to the detriment of aesthetics. However, this doesn't have to be the case. So how do we find that balance between form and function? You can incorporate functionality and practicality into your home while still ensuring that your home looks and feels really beautiful.

Storage

Functionality helps maximise all available space and ensures that your home serves a purpose, is multifunctional and feels nice to be in.

If you read any real estate blurb for a house or apartment you're considering purchasing, you'll notice that any place with plenty of storage has this emphasised in the sales pitch. You'll find it's usually right at the top of the house hunter's wish list, too.

Storage can be added to most homes with a bit of thought and doesn't have to be something you spend thousands of dollars on. There are lots of clever ways to add storage when you're on a budget, but there are also plenty of ways to invest money. Built-in pieces that are custom-made to fit within your home is an expense you need to budget for, but it also adds value to your home, which you will get back tenfold if you ever sell.

We all know the struggles of knowing you own an item you desperately need but can't locate because your storage facilities have let you down. There's nothing worse than knowing you own a specific pair of shoes that'll complete your outfit perfectly but you're running late for work and can't find them anywhere. This is where functionality comes in. If you had a dedicated shoe cabinet built into your wardrobe, you would know exactly where every shoe you owned was located and it would make getting dressed each morning a lot less stressful.

Good storage clears up floor space, makes smart use of the existing space you have, supports activities you do daily, reduces clutter and stress, and makes your home much more visually appealing.

There are plenty of ways to add storage to your home, including built-in joinery, shelving, dressers, baskets and bins, wardrobes and armoires, trays and so much more.

The magic of trays. They can organise your junk in a second. Put a tray anywhere where you've got things you need easy access to but which can't be neatly corralled on their own.

Furniture placement, floor plans and traffic flow

When planning your furniture placement and floor-plan layout, there are some important elements to consider.

- Movement
- Leisure/rest

- Work/task
- Storage

These are the elements you need to consider and they will be referred to often in the discussions about individual rooms in the third section of this book.

Not all of these elements are always required. Sometimes a room is purely for work such as a home office or study, or a room is purely for leisure such as a media room or pool room. Some furniture is multifunctional, which can solve two elements in one; for example, a desk with plenty of built-in storage.

PROPORTIONS

The size of your furniture is possibly the biggest contributor to giving the illusion of space, but choosing it creates a massive amount of anxiety. What if you get the sofa size wrong? There's no inexpensive way to undo that kind of mistake.

Following the floor plans provided for each room will help you work out the correct size of furniture so you can confidently walk into a furniture store and purchase a big-ticket item without too much anxiety.

Arranging your furniture to allow for easy movement to doorways or focal points ensures that people can easily manoeuvre around the room or children can happily play without bumping into things.

When mapping out your floor plan you need to take the following steps.

1 Measure the walls.

2 Measure any furniture you're keeping.

3 Measure doors and windows.

4 Map out traffic flow.

5 Draw up using computer-aided software such as SketchUp, Morpholio Trace or FloorPlanner, or go old school with pen and graph paper.

Think about how you live. Children and pets use a room very differently from adults. They're also a lot lower to the ground and more likely to bump into things.

Ergonomics

Ergonomics focus heavily on comfort and support, from the correct heights for chairs and tables to desk sizing and shapes to ensure that your working environment will support long-term use.

When thinking about ergonomics, the image that is conjured up can be ugly but practical office chairs. That doesn't have to be the case. If you get the comfort levels right and find ways to make the items more attractive, you've found that balance between form and function.

Ergonomics apply to all aspects of your home, from the height of your kitchen bench to finding the perfect spot for the toilet roll. Throughout this book you'll find illustrations and diagrams that show you the ideal dimensions needed to achieve ergonomic success. These will minimise daily struggles and make it easier to perform day-to-day tasks, while making your home more visually appealing and efficient.

Sound dampening

Walking through an empty home you'll hear your footsteps and your voice echo around the rooms. Have you ever noticed that after you've moved in that echo-y sound sometimes still persists?

It is most likely due to not having enough sound-dampening textures and materials around the room to absorb the harsh sounds.

Have you ever seen foam stuck to the bottom of a cafe or restaurant table? It's to help absorb sound and stop echoing or clanging cutlery and crockery. However, before you go investing in expensive sound absorption foam for your ceiling or panels for your walls, there are a number of things you can do or change within the existing room to help make the echo quieter.

You can use similar tricks to quieten a loud room, especially if it's a room little children or pets are running through, and you want to keep their noise to a minimum.

There are different ways of absorbing sound.

TEXTILES: Curtains, cushions, throw rugs, canvas artworks and tablecloths make excellent sound dampeners.

RUGS: Not just useful to muffle footfall, rugs are great sound absorbers. Opt for 100 per cent wool for the best impact. Carpeting a room also helps with this, too.

DECOR ITEMS: Bookshelves full of books are particularly useful for absorbing sound.

PLANTS: They can help break up sound in a room while also creating a more pleasant environment.

There are also items that create annoying acoustics and are worth limiting in your home.

- Glass-topped furniture
- Marble, concrete and stone furniture
- Metal furniture and lamp bases
- Glass-fronted cabinets and bookshelves
- Mirrored surfaces

Accessibility

A beautiful room isn't any good to anyone if you can't actually use it properly. Accessibility is a key element to consider when planning your home, and not just in terms of the floor-plan layout. Armchair height, types of sofa arms, grab rails and more all need to be factored into the way homes are designed.

Accessibility is especially important for children, people with disabilities, elderly people and those who suffer from mobility issues. Pay careful attention to incorporating small changes that have a huge impact on accessibility, such as grab rails, wider doorways and ramped entries into showers.

Opt for handles instead of knobs for cabinets, and levers instead of knobs for doors. Levers are better for accessibility. Knobs are harder to turn for people with mobility issues or when opening doors with full or wet hands.

The height of your door handles matters, too. In the 1900s, they were a lot lower than now. In the 1920s they were three-quarters of the way up the door, which is often the first giveaway of the age of your home. It can be tough going for children under a certain age to open these doors. (Some parents would argue that's a great benefit!)

There are other accessibility elements to consider.

FLOORING: Non-slip flooring in wet areas like bathrooms and kitchens helps to avoid accidents.

SMART TECHNOLOGY: Great for turning lights on and off and controlling underfloor heating and air-conditioning, and they can also be voice-activated.

MOTION SENSOR LIGHTING: Not just good for security reasons at night but also helps the family move around the home after lights are out. Children can make it to the bathroom without any monsters scaring them on the way.

Privacy

An element most homeowners and renters want to incorporate into their homes is keeping certain areas private and out of view from passers-by on the streets. Window treatments are the best way to solve any issues of privacy but another option worth considering is translucent film on any glass windows facing onto a road or pathway that you don't want people to be able to see through.

Homes not only need to be shielded from strangers on the street, it's also important to be able to be private within your home. Bathrooms, bedrooms and wardrobes are the obvious ones. Installing privacy locks on these doors stops you from feeling exposed and creates boundaries.

Multifunctional furniture

Short on storage space? Multifunctional pieces of furniture give you practical solutions for optimising your storage, reduce clutter, make it easier to find things and allow your furniture to adapt to changes to your lifestyle or family structure.

Items such as sofa beds, extension tables, storage ottomans, gas-lift storage beds, modular sofas that can be rearranged, nesting tables and Murphy beds give you loads of flexibility and functionality if built-in storage or extra beds for guests are in short supply!

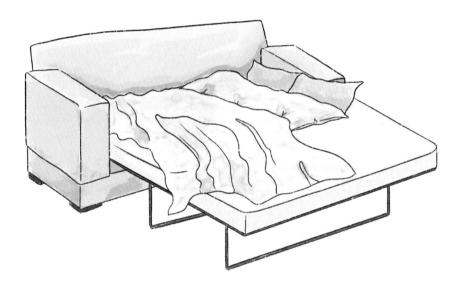

Lighting

Lighting will be covered throughout the book but it's worth calling out its functionality at this point because it's such an important element in building, creating or decorating a home.

There are a lot of different ways to light your home and they are not just from the ceiling.

- Natural light through the windows and doors

- Reading lights by your bedside or sofa

- Task lighting for your desk or above the kitchen bench

- Accent lights to add to the overall light levels

- Atmosphere and mood lighting for evenings when you're entertaining or want to watch a movie on the couch with a loved one

- Architectural elements that not only provide you with additional light for the room but also become a striking talking piece

What type of lighting should you plan for your home? There are three types of light you should think about.

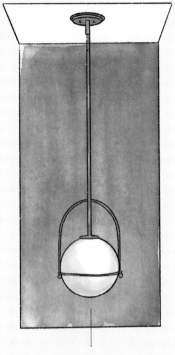

DIRECT LIGHT:

Overhead pendants, floor lamps,
wall spots and table lamps

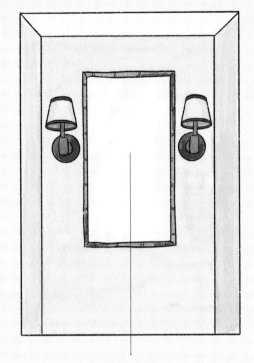

INDIRECT LIGHT:

Wall sconces, oyster/ceiling mounted
and chandeliers

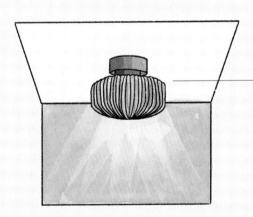

DIFFUSED LIGHT:

Glass shades, and fabric or washi paper
shades to soften harsh light

Creating
the rooms

THERE IS TRUE MAGIC
IN INTENTIONALLY CRAFTING
A BEAUTIFUL ROOM TO ENJOY.

WELCOMING

Why hello there! Come on in!

First impressions count and the minute your door is opened impressions start forming. Your entryway is one of the hardest working rooms in the house and can be a tricky space to get right. Why? Well, when you think about it, it serves so many purposes. However, its biggest challenge is the fact that it's a highly functional space that also needs to look inviting and give a nod to what your guests may find as they continue through your home. (And don't forget what the courier sees when they come to deliver your online shopping orders!) Since the room packs a double punch, it means twice the amount of effort for you when planning the design. It's also a thoroughfare so it can't be too cluttered or it becomes an obstacle for everyone who lives there.

You don't need a lot of furniture, but it does need to work well for you. Embracing the optical illusion of a mirror and its ability to reflect light and make a space feel brighter will help greatly when planning your entryway. And a console table or sideboard that offers a place to do your stop and drop when you come home each day is also useful. The decorative layers come in the form of artwork, table lamps and decor.

Hallway hero

Everyone loves a talking point! Your hero piece is something to comment on as your guests walk in. It may not necessarily be a piece of furniture or decor given that your hallway is usually a narrow space that you pass through rather than see front on. It may be a fantastic view out to a bush setting or a picture window framing a gorgeous section of the swimming pool.

If you don't have the luxury of an incredible view to frame, then you do have the opportunity to make the focal point your console table or a stunning artwork lit up by a beautiful wall sconce.

Here are some ideas for your hallway hero.

- A large artwork in a bold colour
- A striking mirror
- An eye-catching wallpaper
- An incredible staircase with a hanging chandelier
- Impressive wall sconces lighting up the entryway

Furniture

Below is a list of furniture pieces that you would typically use to furnish and style a hallway or entryway.

CONSOLE TABLE

This is a long, narrow table placed against the wall where you can drop keys or the mail on your way in. Tables often have a narrow drawer for small storage.

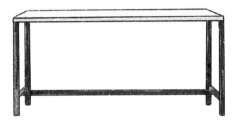

SIZE GUIDE: Approximately 130–150 cm W × 30 cm D × 80 cm H (51–59 × 16 × 31 in)

BUFFETS AND SIDEBOARDS

If storage is an issue in your home, a buffet or sideboard acts as additional storage space for your shoes, bags, hats and other paraphernalia you might want on hand by the front door.

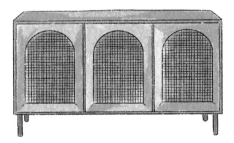

SIZE GUIDE: Approximately 160–180 cm W × 40–50 cm D × 70–90 cm H (59–70 × 27–35 in)

ARTWORK

Adding something to the wall brings your eyes up to make the room appear taller. Art gives you the opportunity to let your personality shine through. Perhaps you're an amateur photographer and you'd like to display some of your own handiwork. Or maybe you have inherited a beautiful piece of art that needs reframing to fit your home's aesthetic.

SIZE GUIDE: Entirely dependent on the piece itself but if you're hanging a piece of art above a console or sideboard, you'll want it to be about three-quarters of the size of the piece of furniture underneath it.

BENCH SEAT

A convenient spot to sit and take your shoes on and off.

SIZE GUIDE: From 100 cm W × 35 cm D × 45 cm H (39 × 14 × 18 in)

COAT RACK

Don't have space for large pieces of furniture? Perhaps a coat rack or hooks are a good alternative to give you some storage solutions without filling the walkway.

SHOE CUPBOARD

Keep your entryway clutter-free by having a dedicated storage solution for shoes.

UMBRELLA STAND

A stand for your umbrellas is handy to have stored by the door,

MIRROR

Depending on your preference, hanging a mirror above the console table is a great spot for a last check before you head out the door. If you'd prefer to add colour or texture to the room instead, opt for an artwork as your feature.

SIZE GUIDE: Round or square mirrors 80–100 cm D (31–39 in); rectangular mirrors from 100 cm W × 80 cm H (39 × 31 in).

HALL RUNNER

Long skinny rugs placed down the length of the hallway suit narrow hallways. They help to muffle footfall, as well as adding colour, texture or pattern to the space.

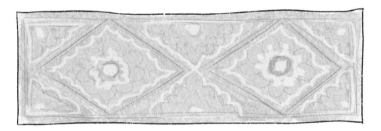

SIZE GUIDE: From 75 cm W × 300 cm L (30 × 118 in)

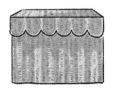

STORAGE BASKETS

Often placed under the console table to stay out of the way of the hallway, storage baskets can be used for shoes, school bags and other accessories.

ART WALL LIGHT

A common addition to a hallway where natural light is limited, a wall washer light or gallery wall light allows you to direct the light specifically on a piece of artwork or object you have mounted on the wall.

PLANTS

A little potted plant on the console table or a taller indoor plant as your hero piece is a nice injection of life at your front door.

DECORATIVE ITEMS

A stack of books, a scented candle you can light just before your guests come over, a vase full of beautiful, picked flowers from your garden or a tray for keeping your keys organised will enhance the table.

Floor plans

Entryways are tricky spaces because you're usually just transitioning through. However, it's important that the entryway is its own space, fulfilling a practical need but also giving you the chance to welcome your guests with a beautiful artwork, mirror or statement pendant light.

LONG NARROW CORRIDOR

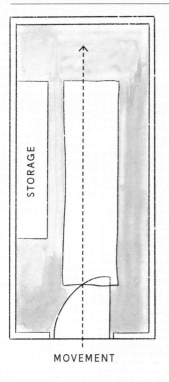

STORAGE

MOVEMENT

WIDE OPEN SQUARE SPACE

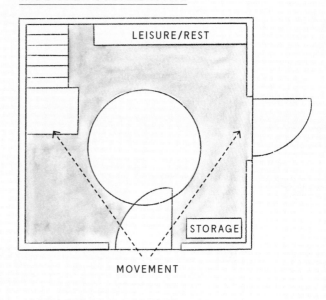

LEISURE/REST

STORAGE

MOVEMENT

Question: Which side do you place furniture down a long narrow hallway?

Answer: The furniture goes in line with the door, if possible, so that there is a clear path without the obstacle of a door as you come into the room.

Styling guide

The following illustrations provide some helpful layouts you could consider for your entryway. Use your own creativitiy to help pull together the specific styling pieces. Choose which vignette best suits your space and have some fun with it!

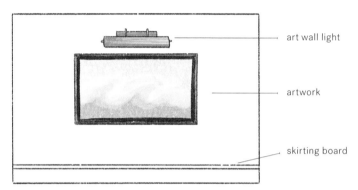

art wall light

artwork

skirting board

ART + WALL LIGHT ABOVE

mud room-style bench seat

ART + BENCH SEAT + CUSHION + POT & PLANT

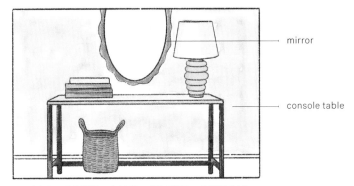

mirror

console table

MIRROR + BOOKS + LAMP + BASKET + CONSOLE

chair

console table

CONSOLE + ART + LAMP + ART FRAMES + CHAIR

buffet table

BUFFET + ART COLLECTION

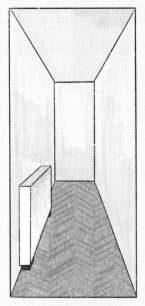

FUNCTION

FOCAL POINT

REFLECTIVITY

LIGHTING

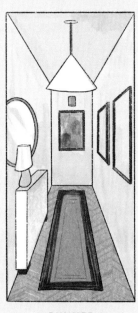

RUNNER

DECOR

Troubleshooting

NARROW ENTRYWAYS

Entryways are typically quite narrow spaces. They're often rectangular in shape with the front door opening into the floor space, limiting usable space. Narrow spaces mean you need to plan every bit of floor real estate. A narrow console table gives you a flat surface to use for storage as well as styling. Or if you really can't spare the floor space, artwork hung on the wall and lit with a wall light means you get impact by the front door without stealing any of the floor.

STORAGE

Storage is at a premium in an entryway. So think of clever storage solutions to house all the paraphernalia that you come through the door with each day, such as school bags, dog leashes, raincoats, keys, children in strollers, parcels, bags of groceries and so on. Think about what furniture pieces can help make this a more practical spot, such as baskets, pull-out drawers and lift-up bench seats for shoe storage.

SMALL SPACES

Making a small space look larger is always a challenge but using mirrors and floorboards running down the hall, and not across, can change this. The same rule applies to a hall runner, which helps draw the eye down a long passageway and accentuates the space.

FLOORING

Hallways are thoroughfares with high foot traffic so whatever you place on the floor needs to be hardwearing. Opt for tiles in an entryway as they can take quite a beating before showing signs of wear and tear, whereas floorboards scuff and scratch a lot faster.

SITTING

Your lounge room is the hub of the home. Maybe that's always been said about the kitchen but it could be time to update that old saying considering how hard living spaces work. The lounge room is the connection point to every other room in the house, with most rooms feeding off it. It provides a range of different uses, including relaxation after a long day at work, social interaction when entertaining friends and family, entertainment for children playing video games or hosting board game nights, connection with household members and quality bonding time, plus so much more.

If the home is a sanctuary where people retreat for shelter and safety, then surely the lounge room is up there as one of the most important rooms in the house when renovating or decorating. It is also the most likely room to be seen and used by guests. Many people place the lounge room at the top of the list when deciding which rooms to invest the most time, money and effort. This is where you can easily tip into overthinking mode because of the pressure to get the room right.

By following the elements of styling and utilising the floor-plan ideas, you'll enjoy a new found sense of confidence when designing your lounge room space.

Lounge room hero

Your sofa is the hardest working item in your lounge room and should be what you purchase first and where you allocate most of your budget. There are some sofa purchasing tips to keep in mind when shopping.

It's what's inside that counts. Look for quality features such as foam inserts with feather wrapped around the block of foam that will give you support as well as comfort.

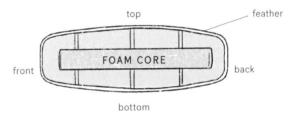

The depth of your sofa is one of the biggest contributors to comfort. If you get a sofa that's too deep, it will be difficult to put your feet flat on the ground when seated. If it's too shallow, it won't be comfortable to lounge around on as you'll feel you're being forced forward by the back cushions. The average sofa depth is around 90–100 cm (35–39 in).

Seat height is important, especially if you're tall or have a long torso. Many of the more modern sofa styles are quite low to the ground, which is not ideal for the ageing population who require more lumbar support. Average sofa height is around 85–95 cm (33–37 in) but it's important to look at seat height, too. Most sofas sit at around 40 cm (16 in) off the ground, but if you want more support aim for 50 cm (20 in).

MID CENTURY

BUTTON BACK SOFA

CAMEL BACK

CHESTERFIELD

SLIPCOVER

ENGLISH ROLL-ARM

ART DECO

1970S

MODULAR

CHAISE SOFA

Choose an appropriate style of sofa for your home. Such a large piece of furniture is one of the first indicators of the style of the room. If you've chosen a sofa with a skirt and tailored back cushions then you've got a more formal, classic style going on. If you want to give a more modern, relaxed vibe, you'll want to choose a sofa that sits lower to the ground with floppy cushions that you sink into.

The colour of your sofa matters. Ideally you want it to last seven to ten years, so thinking about the fabric choice and colour is important. If you're wanting to go with a safer option that will last numerous cushion, rug or art upgrades, opt for a neutral fabric like a sandy beige or a charcoal grey. They're far less likely to stand out when you want to upgrade other elements in the room. If you're ready to make a bit more of a statement but not bold enough to go with hot pink, then consider navy, olive green, deep burgundy or teal – striking enough to stand out but not so much of a risk that they determine your future colour palette options.

Know your limits when it comes to maximum dimensions. If you measure out your ideal sofa size well in advance, you'll know what you can seriously consider when out shopping. This will avoid making an expensive mistake with furniture that doesn't fit in your house (or worse still, doesn't fit through the door or in your elevator). So measure your doorways and elevators before you start shopping!)

Measure the diagonal dimensions of your sofa so you can turn it sideways or stand it upright if you're worried about it fitting through the door.

Furniture

SOFA

The sofa is the biggest purchase you will make for your lounge room. The size you need will differ from home to home and many sofas can be custom tailored specifically to the size you need. Generally, you want your sofa to take up about two-thirds of the wall it's sitting against.

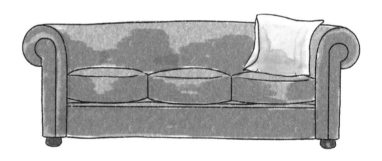

SIZE GUIDE: 2-seater sofas 150 cm W × 85 cm D × 90 cm H (59 × 33 × 35 in)

SIZE GUIDE: 3-seater sofas 180 cm W × 85 cm D × 90 cm H (71 × 33 × 35 in)

SIZE GUIDE: 3.5-seater sofas 220 cm W × 85 cm D × 90 cm H (87 × 33 × 35 in)

SIZE GUIDE: 4-seater sofas 250 cm W × 85 cm D × 90 cm H (98 × 33 × 35 in)

TV UNITS AND ENTERTAINMENT UNITS

These are forever upgrading in size to match ever-growing TV sizes. Ideally, the length of your TV unit should be a few inches larger than the TV sitting above it to allow for the proportions to work well.

SIZE GUIDE: 150–220 cm W × 45 cm D × 45 cm H (59–87 × 18 × 18 in)

ROUND COFFEE TABLES

Best for allowing ease of movement around a room. They don't have sharp edges your shins bang into and they're not going to hurt as much if children bump their heads into them when rushing around.

SIZE GUIDE: 80–120 cm D (31–47 in)

RECTANGULAR COFFEE TABLES

Good for long narrow spaces that don't have a lot of room for traffic flow. Generally, you want a rectangular coffee table to sit about two-thirds of the length of your sofa.

SIZE GUIDE: 120 cm W × 40 cm D × 35 cm H (47 × 16 × 14 in)

SIDE TABLES: They can vary from rectangular to round and are great additional tables for a water glass or table lamp.

SIZE GUIDE: 45 cm W × 45 cm D × 50 cm H (18 × 18 × 20 in)

ARMCHAIRS OR OCCASIONAL CHAIRS

Add comfort and functionality to your lounge room as an additional spot to sit, as well as adding a feature to the room in a pattern or colour. They can be grouped in pairs to create symmetry or used alone to create a cosy reading nook.

SIZE GUIDE: 70 cm W × 75 cm D × 75 cm H (28 × 30 × 30 in)

OTTOMANS

Great versatile pieces that can be used as extra seating or for resting your feet on while sitting on the sofa.

SIZE GUIDE: 55 cm W × 50 cm D × 38 cm H (22 × 20 × 15 in)

Floor plans

Your sofa is usually the largest piece of furniture in the room, so working out its placement first helps the rest of the room come together. The following floor plans will help maximise your lounge room space, balance proportions and make a comfortable living space.

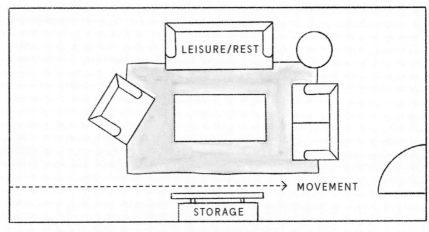

TV FOCUSED

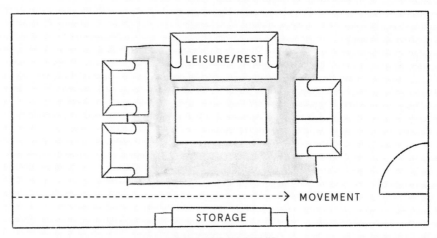

FIREPLACE FOCUSED

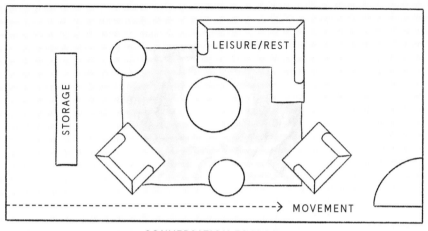

CONVERSATION FOCUSED

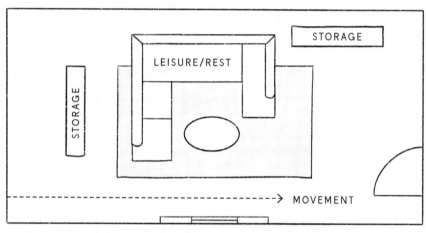

VIEW FOCUSED

TV TO COFFEE TABLE: 60-80 cm (24-31 in)

COFFEE TABLE TO SOFA: 60-80 cm (24-31 in)

WIDTH: Your coffee table length should be approximately half to three-quarters of the sofa length.

HEIGHT: Your coffee table should be the same height or slightly lower than the sofa, never higher.

The gap from the sofa to the coffee table should be about 40-80 cm (16-31 in). Close enough to reach across to grab your glass.

Style Your Home

Styling guide

Ever wondered how the professionals get their styling so right? They picture an invisible triangle when styling a flat surface to help map out which items should go where. The top of the triangle is where the highest or tallest items are placed and then everything else sits nicely within the triangle from there. See the illustration for a visual representation.

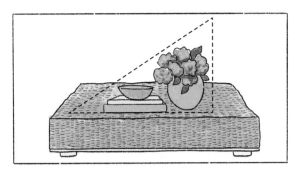

Keep in mind that the best flat lays are the ones that look the most effortless, and sometimes that takes time to create. You won't necessarily nail it the first time you try.

Use these styling tips to help map out your coffee table, fireplace or bookcase and, most importantly, have a little fun with it!

ELEMENTS TO USE

Vary the height, shape, size and visual weight of the items you choose for your tabletop. You'll want tall items, short items, greenery, a tray to corral the items and some objects of art for interest. You could include:

- Flowers
- Heirlooms
- Books
- Candles
- Trays

- Plants
- Trinkets
- Bowls
- Coasters
- Seasonal decor

- Matches
- Vases
- Found objects
- Crystals

STYLING THE COFFEE TABLE

Flat-lay styling can be tricky. The key to styling your coffee table is balance. Use the triangle diagram to help you determine which pieces need to sit on your table.

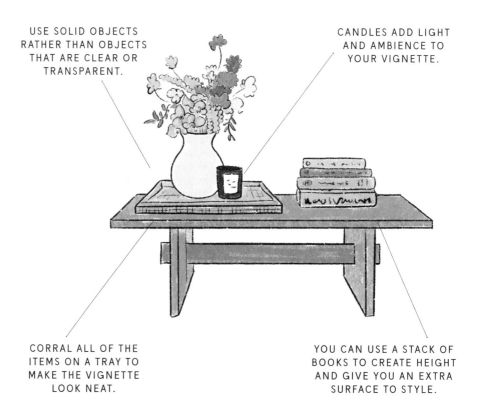

USE SOLID OBJECTS RATHER THAN OBJECTS THAT ARE CLEAR OR TRANSPARENT.

CANDLES ADD LIGHT AND AMBIENCE TO YOUR VIGNETTE.

CORRAL ALL OF THE ITEMS ON A TRAY TO MAKE THE VIGNETTE LOOK NEAT.

YOU CAN USE A STACK OF BOOKS TO CREATE HEIGHT AND GIVE YOU AN EXTRA SURFACE TO STYLE.

STYLING THE FIREPLACE

The first step is to map out your focal point. Choose from any of the following anchor ideas and follow the diagrams to execute the styling yourself.

MIRROR

ART

CLOCK

TV

SHELVING

STYLING THE SOFA

Not sure how to coordinate your sofa cushions to make them look cohesive? The key here is to use the elements of styling in terms of contrast, texture and size. Don't opt for the same cushion on repeat; rather try varying the textures on the sofa for interest. For example, you could choose a beautiful, printed linen and pair it with an opulent velvet-feel fabric. Alternate the placement of square cushions and lumbar cushions on the sofa or bundle them together to style them in an inviting way.

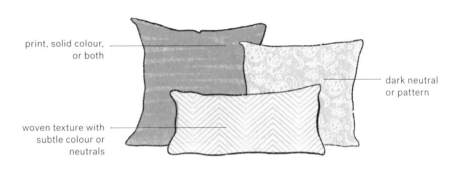

print, solid colour, or both

dark neutral or pattern

woven texture with subtle colour or neutrals

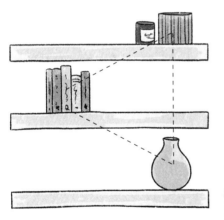

STYLING THE BOOKSHELF

Again, apply the triangle rule to each shelf or use it as the overall anchor to help you determine where to place items. Your bookcase doesn't have to be only for books; you can use it to show off some of your styling prowess with vases, photo frames, candles and more.

The key to successful styling is allowing for breathing space. Refer back to the balance element (page 50) to remind yourself about how to achieve this.

STYLING THE WINDOWS

Your lounge room windows have a multitude of uses, including light filtering and providing privacy, sound absorption and decoration.

Depending on your needs and requirements, opt for sheers for light filtering and some privacy. If you get a lot of sun you need to block or dilute in summer months, or if you want to black out the room entirely for watching movies, you'll need a combo of sheers and blockouts.

Hang curtains carefully around windows. Bulky fabric either side of your window won't help with the illusion of a spacious room, nor will really heavyweight fabric. Keep the fabric lighter and sheer for smaller spaces where you need to create an illusion of space.

Curtains in your lounge room can give a multitude of different effects.

- Add height, texture, colour and pattern

- Soften a room full of harsh elements, such as concrete and glass

- Absorb sound in a large open space

- Provide privacy

- Filter light and regulate temperature

- Draw attention to and frame a beautiful view

- Give a sense of elegance to the room

DOS AND DON'TS

- If you're looking for a more traditional classic look, then puddling the curtains on the ground is something you could consider.

- When deciding on curtain width, a general rule of thumb is to make the curtain half as wide again as the width of your window. For example, if your window is 2 m (7 ft) wide, your curtains will be 3 m (10 ft) wide.

- Hang the rod or track from the ceiling or as close to the ceiling as possible, and not directly above the window frame. This will draw your eye up and make the room feel taller and more elegant.

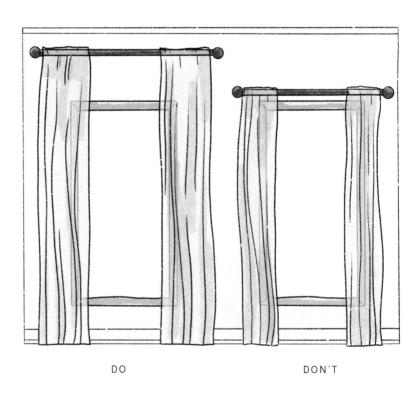

DO   DON'T

Troubleshooting

FILLING A LARGE OPEN-PLAN SPACE

- Open-plan spaces can be one of the trickiest spaces to furnish. When working with a rectangular space with only one function, it's easier to determine the layout of the room. For example, the longest wall is generally where the sofa goes or the dining table is usually centred. When working with a large space that has multiple functions and a huge amount of floor space, you need to be smart about the way you place your furniture.

- Use furniture to zone off space. Rugs also help significantly by signalling where a space starts and stops. Rugs under dining tables and sofas instantly differentiate the dining zone and TV or sitting zone in the room.

- Keep in mind it's not a ballroom. Start in the centre and move out. You don't need to place all your furniture against every wall. It'll make the space feel weird if the seating is on opposite sides of the room. If you've got loads of space, start by placing your furniture in the middle of the room and work your way out.

- Lighting is a huge consideration as you'll either need to light from above (ceiling mounted) or install powerpoints in your floors to allow for table lamps and floor lamps in the middle of the room. Wall sconces help light the sides of the room so a careful combo of lights above, at floor level and on side walls means you can control the mood lighting.

- Don't forget the acoustics. Large rooms echo, so textiles are your friends when it comes to dampening loud noises.

CHOOSING A RUG

Determining the correctly sized rug to purchase, as well as where to place it in the room, can cause anxiety. Here are some helpful hints to think about when shopping for your lounge room rug.

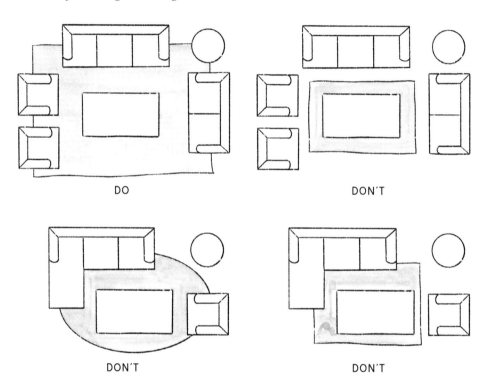

DO   DON'T

DON'T   DON'T

- Ideally, you want 30–50 cm (12–20 in) of rug showing on either side of your sofa.

- Where possible, place all the front feet of your furniture on top of your rug.

- Centre the rug in the room or against the sofa to help give even proportions to the room.

- Vary the texture of your sofa and your rug. Don't choose similar textures or there won't be enough contrast in the room to make it interesting.

- Don't pick a rug in a similar colour to your sofa because it will look like a big blob of one colour in a large space.

- Don't clash your rug pattern and sofa pattern. It's usually a better idea to choose a solid colour sofa and patterned rug (or vice versa) so that the patterns in your room are not competing with each other for attention.

SOFA CUSHIONS

The most beautiful lounge room can be let down instantly by sad-looking cushions sitting on the sofa. No one likes pancake-flat scatter cushions. They're not comfortable and they look tired when they've been squished down. Avoid this by upsizing your cushion inserts to a size larger than your cushion cover. That way they'll keep their shape much longer and be far more comfortable to sit against.

40 × 40 cm (16 in × 16 in) cushion cover

50 × 50 cm (20 in × 20 in) cushion insert

50 × 50 (20 in × 20 in) cushion cover

60 × 60 cm (24 in × 24 in) cushion insert

60 × 60 (24 in × 24 in) cushion cover

70 × 70 cm (28 in × 28 in) cushion insert

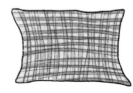

40 × 60cm (16 in × 24 in) cushion cover

50 × 70 cm (20 in × 28 in) cushion insert

You can style your cushions in different ways.

SYMMETRICALLY: Two either side

AS A TRIO: Two square cushions in each corner with one lumbar cushion

ASYMMETRICALLY: Odd groupings of cushions filling up the entire sofa

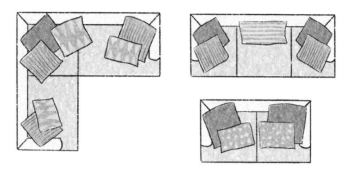

TABLES

Your coffee table should be slightly lower than your sofa seat. This makes it easier to place glasses or food platters (or your feet!) on the table and doesn't create a barrier to any other seating in the room, which could restrict conversation.

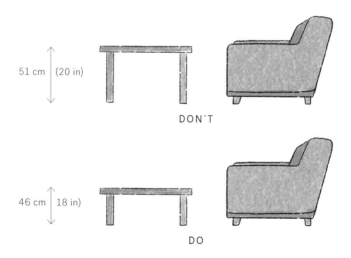

51 cm (20 in)

DON'T

46 cm 18 in)

DO

MOUNTING THE TV

Getting the height of your TV right means much more enjoyable viewing. Follow the diagram below to determine the correct height for your TV.

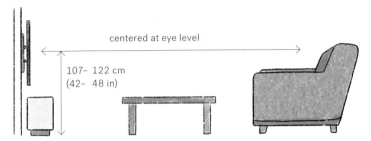

centered at eye level

107– 122 cm
(42– 48 in)

If you're mounting the TV above a fireplace, you'll probably need to hang it a little higher than you would if it was a blank wall, depending on how high your fireplace sits.

If you're building or renovating, you can determine the TV height sweet spot before you install a fireplace so it can all work in proportion.

DO

DON'T

HANGING ART

If you think about it, the majority of the items in your home – sofas, tables, desks, chairs, side tables, coffee tables and sideboards – are not much taller than 1 metre. So you can use art to help fill the empty space between the top of your furniture and the ceiling.

Many people get the height of their artworks wrong and then the whole room looks out of proportion. These guidelines will help you determine their correct height.

HANGING ART ON A WALL ON ITS OWN WITH NO FURNITURE UNDERNEATH: 160 cm (63 in) from the floor to the centre of the artwork

HANGING ART ABOVE A PIECE OF FURNITURE: 10–20 cm (4–8 in) between the bottom of the piece of art and furniture

GALLERY WALL GAPS BETWEEN FRAMES: 5–10 cm (2–4 in) between each piece of art

GALLERY WALLS

The key to keeping gallery walls looking classy is to find a common element and repeat it throughout. For example, keep all frames the same but vary the sizes, or have the same-sized frames or keep all photos/prints in black and white.

When hanging art:

- Cut newspaper to the size of your frame and tape it to the wall to help visualise it.

- Place the artworks out on the floor first to make the right arrangement so you can see how they'll all work together.

Not only is the height of your artwork important, but picking the right-sized art for a space in the first place is half the battle won.

The art should be three-quarters of the size of the piece of furniture below it. That way it'll give nice scale and look in proportion to the room. If three-quarters feels too large for you or you don't have the perfect piece, you can go down to two-thirds without losing impact.

Renting and can't put holes in the walls? Use these tips!

- If you wanted to hang an artwork above a console or sideboard, just rest it against the wall instead. You'll still get the impact of the artwork but won't have a hole in the wall.

- Use 3M sticky hooks. They work well for lighter-weight pieces such as framed posters or canvases rather than framed prints and framed canvases that can be quite heavy.

EATING

Once dining rooms had their own room in the house. These days they're more often integrated into open-plan spaces in lounge rooms and kitchens to give homes an open and breezy feel, which is much more conducive for entertaining, socialising and family interaction.

In an age where technology is a big distraction and often means lack of interaction, being able to come together around the dining table holds great significance. This is where family traditions, stories and recipes are passed on to the next generation, so it makes sense to invest in the items you place in this space.

For children, the dining room is a place of routine, connection and sharing (or at least learning to share with their siblings). It's a place of gathering where stories are swapped about what happened at school that day, life concerns are discussed and, of course, table manners and correct table etiquette is learnt.

Nowadays, dining rooms are multifunctional spaces that are more than just a space for eating meals. They can be transformed into workspaces, homework stations, craft tables and family game night tables. The room will no doubt continue to evolve over the coming years but it is clear that your dining table is an extremely significant item in your home.

Dining hero

It's not surprising that the hero piece for this chapter is the dining table. For some people, their childhood dining table is so dear that they could tell you the direction of every timber grain from tracing it with their cutlery at dinner time each evening. It's also funny to note that most people have a preferred spot at the table and if someone else sits in their seat without knowing, it can cause mayhem!

ROUND OR RECTANGULAR?

Usually this comes down to personal preference or size restraints. Round dining tables are great for fostering intimacy as they encourage conversation with almost everyone at the table because you can easily make eye contact. They're also a lot easier for people to manoeuvre around as there are no sharp edges. This is great for families with children who zoom around and are right at table bumping height.

The other great benefit you get from a round table is that there's no head of the table, so moving chairs is easy and creates a more inclusive feel. And lastly, their more organic shape means they slot nicely into a smaller corner of the room if you don't have a tonne of space available for seating.

Furniture

DINING TABLE

There are a number of different shapes available when it comes to dining tables – round, square, oval and rectangular.

OVAL/RECTANGULAR DINING TABLES (BY LENGTH)

SIZE GUIDE: 160–180 cm (63–71 in) = 4 people

SIZE GUIDE: 200–220 cm (79–87 in) = 6 people

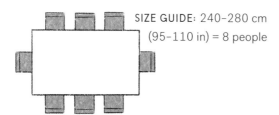

SIZE GUIDE: 240–280 cm (95–110 in) = 8 people

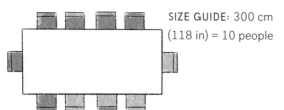

SIZE GUIDE: 300 cm (118 in) = 10 people

ROUND DINING TABLES (BY DIAMETER)

SIZE GUIDE: under 90 cm (35 in) = 2 people

SIZE GUIDE: 90–100 cm (35–39 in) = 3 people

SIZE GUIDE: 120 cm (47 in) = 4 people

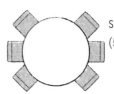

SIZE GUIDE: 150 cm (59 in) = 6 people

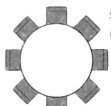

SIZE GUIDE: 180 cm (71 in) = 8 people

DINING CHAIRS

Comfort is key when choosing dining chairs so that you're not wishing for the meal to be over because you want to sit somewhere more comfortable. If you want to take a risk with some colour or pattern, an upholstered dining chair can add to the personality of your room. Think of your dining chairs as just as much of an investment as your table.

SIZE GUIDE: 45 cm W × 45 cm D × 80 cm H; seat height: 45 cm (18 × 18 × 31 in; seat height: 18 in)

SIDEBOARD AND BUFFET

If you have the luxury of space, a key piece in your dining room is a sideboard or buffet to keep overflow crockery, cutlery or less frequently used serving platters. They're a great spot for napkins, placemats and coasters so they're within easy reach of the table.

SIZE GUIDE: From 180 cm W × 45 cm D × 90 cm H (71 × 18 × 35 in)

ART

Whether it's a large statement piece of art on the wall behind the table or a decorative objet d'art, you need something beautiful and striking in your dining room.

SIZE GUIDE: This depends on where the artwork is being hung. Remember the three-quarters or two-thirds rule from the previous chapter? The same rule can be applied to the dining room.

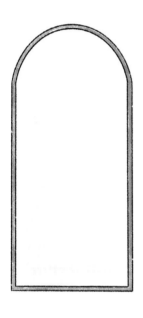

MIRRORS

In place of an artwork, mirrors are a great option to help bounce more light back into the room when opposite a window or hanging pendant. It can be a statement mirror or something relatively simple in design, but either will enhance the light levels in the room.

SIZE GUIDE: Depending on the size of your table, you'll want your mirror to be smaller by at least 20 per cent. For example, if your table is 200 cm (79 in) in length, you wouldn't want the mirror to be any longer than 180 cm (71 in). Go for a round mirror when you've got a smaller dining table.

TABLE LAMPS

Mood lighting in your dining room is super important when you're entertaining and want to be able to control the ambience. A table lamp on the sideboard can offer additional light as well as adding colour and fun to your room.

SIZE GUIDE: From 60 cm H (24 in)

FLOOR LAMPS

An easy addition to your dining room, a floor lamp placed in the corner lights up the room and successfully fills an otherwise unused space. Remember to check the diameter of the shade to ensure that it does not overpower the corner.

SIZE GUIDE: From 160–180 cm H (63–71 in)

HANGING PENDANTS

Add instant ambience, sophistication and proportion to your dining room by hanging a pendant light above the table. By having an item hanging from the ceiling down to the table, your eye is drawn up to the ceiling, which tricks your eye into thinking it is higher than it really is.

SIZE GUIDE: This will depend on a number of factors; however, the following gudelines should help.

ROUND DINING TABLES: Pick a pendant about 30 cm (12 in) smaller in diameter than the dining table.

RECTANGULAR DINING TABLES: Pick a pendant that measures around half the length of your table (maximum size would be two-thirds of the table).

WALL SCONCES

Wall sconces placed above a buffet or sideboard can be used to light up an artwork or mirror.

BAR CARTS

A common item to be found in many dining rooms, the bar cart is a little drinks trolley that can be moved around the room on wheels. Alternatively, a larger bar cabinet provides storage for bottles of wine and spirits.

ROUND BAR CART: 50 D × 85 cm H (20 × 33 in)

BAR TROLLEY: 80 cm W × 35 cm D × 85 cm H (31 × 14 × 33 in)

BAR CABINET: 100 cm W × 45 cm D × 100 cm H (39 × 18 × 39 in)

Floor plans

The dining table, your central focus in the dining room, can come in different shapes. The following illustrations will help guide you to work out the best placement of furniture.

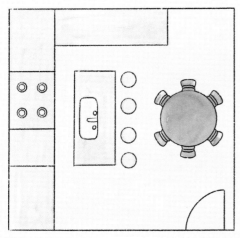

ROUND TABLE

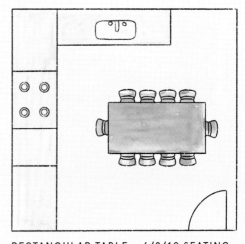

RECTANGULAR TABLE – 6/8/10 SEATING

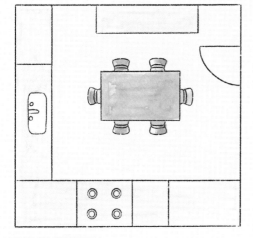

EAT IN KITCHEN

KITCHEN ISLAND DINING

Styling guide

You've got a number of options when styling the middle of your dining table. You can choose one singular item that takes up a large portion of the space, a runner with items dotted down the table or a tray housing smaller objects in the centre.

Troubleshooting

PUSH-OUT SPACE

You should allow for 60–90 cm (24–35 in) of space either side of the table so that you can comfortably push your dining chairs out and stand up. This isn't always possible to achieve but provides you with a good guide when you're planning your room layout.

RUGS UNDER THE TABLE

Do you need a rug under your dining table? Sometimes rugs are more hassle than they're worth because they catch on your dining chairs, collect food scraps and become a tripping hazard when walking around the room. But if you do want a rug under your table, don't choose something that's too thin. Flatweave or really thin rugs will curl up over time, and when pushing your dining chair out to stand up you'll catch the legs on the rug and potentially trip over.

USING A RECTANGULAR TABLE

It may sound counterintuitive but curved edges offer many benefits when it comes to your dining table. Rectangular tables are often very long so can take up quite a large footprint. A round table takes up far less space so can be a good solution for small spaces.

LIGHTING THE TABLE

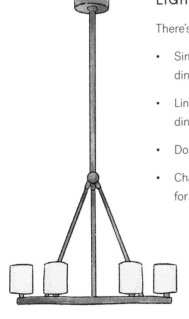

There's an array of lighting options for your dining table.

- Single pendants fixed with a single wire centred on your dining table

- Linear/bar pendants usually fixed in two points above your dining table

- Double pendants fixed equidistant above your dining table

- Chandeliers centred on the dining table in an extra-large size for scale and impact

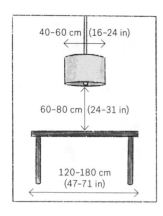

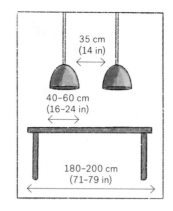

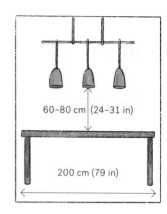

SINGLE PENDANT

- Long table 120–180 cm (47–71 in)

- 1 × 40–60 cm Diameter (16–24 in) pendant

- 60–80 cm (24–31 in) from table to base of light

DOUBLE PENDANT

- Long table 180–200 cm (71–79 in)

- 2 × 40–60 cm W (16–31 in)

- 35 cm (14 in) gap between pendants

TRIPLE PENDANT

- Long table 200 cm (79 in)

- 3 × 60–80 cm (24–31 in) from table to base of light

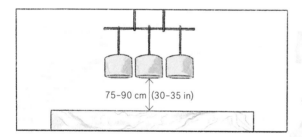

Length of table or island divided by how many pendants you want to hang = distance between each

80 cm (31 in) from table to base of pendant is the ideal height for single and double pendants above a dining table. 75–90 cm (30–35 in) from island bench to pendant light.

Dimmer switches are important in your dining space for a number of reasons. They allow you better control over the light levels in the room, which is handy when you've invited your nearest and dearest over for a winter roast and want to be able to make the room feel moody and cosy. You can start the night with a slightly brighter room and then dim the lights when you get to serving dessert or a post-dinner aperitif.

Style Your Home

SLEEPING

Bedrooms are considered one of the safest spaces in the home. They're the room you think of most when you're away, feeling homesick and wishing you were curled up in your bed under the covers. They represent a space for intimacy, romantic connection, healing, unwinding and relaxing.

Many people expend their efforts on their living and dining spaces and often neglect the bedroom. There are a number of reasons for this, Maybe it's because no one else sees that room apart from the occupants of the home, or you have budget constraints or you focused on the children's bedrooms. Perhaps you've simply run out of puff after spending all your time and energy on the living spaces.

Whatever your reason for neglecting your bedroom, it doesn't need to be that complicated. Bedrooms actually require only a few items to complete them. Since you spend so much of your time in bed, the one non-negotiable is your mattress, but you can certainly pull back on your spending on bedside lamps or decorative cushions.

Where possible, it's always advisable to avoid stimulating elements in your bedroom that might detract from your ability to enjoy restful sleep. But that can't always be guaranteed. You could need to have a little desk, or a treadmill or pilates reformer for exercising because you're short on space. And that's totally fine. You can't always tick every box of your wishlist when setting up a bedroom. It's about getting creative with focus. Perhaps you can buy a bed that's high enough for the reformer to slide underneath or you could opt for calm and soothing colours for the room rather than big bold colours and patterns.

Bedroom hero

Well, this is an obvious one. The bed is the hero in your bedroom, the guest bedroom and your children's bedrooms. Simple!

So what important elements do you need to pay attention to when purchasing a bed? Comfort is the key since you spend so much of your life in bed. Investing in a quality mattress is smart but you also need to get your proportions right so that your room will feel uncluttered and an inviting place where you can relax. Plan a comfortable amount of space either side of the bed so you can easily manoeuvre around the room, open wardrobe doors and bedside drawers, and make the bed.

Determining the placement of the bed is the first challenge and this often dictates what size bed you can fit into the space. You don't want to go into a bedroom and walk straight into the edge of the bed. If you can, place the bed as far away from the door as possible to maximise space. You could choose to face the bed towards a window or set of french doors to take in the view. But if you don't have that luxury, just make sure the doorway into the room is positioned past the end of the bed so you can open the door fully and walk all the way in with ease.

There's no reason why you should have to sacrifice your own bedroom for the sake of other rooms in the house. Budget for your bedroom furniture and styling accessories from the start so you ensure that you're not losing out. It might be a less frequently seen room but that's no reason to completely ignore it.

After you've worked out the bed's placement, the rest of the items all come together a lot more easily.

Your next step is to choose a bed style. Do you want a four-poster bed, an upholstered bedhead, a timber bed frame or do you want to keep it simple with just a bed base? The bed is the biggest piece of furniture in the room so choose a bed that will complement your overall style. You can make the bedhead more interesting by varying the fabrics, textures, shapes and patterns you use, or you can leave it neutral and make other elements such as wallpaper or paint the feature piece in the room.

Don't forget the linen! This is just as important as the bedhead decision. White is an easy option that's timeless, classic and unlikely to date. If you're feeling like you need to inject some more pattern into the house, go for a bolder colour palette or experiment with prints. Then add accessories such as cushions and a throw rug. You can refer to the cushion illustrations on page 126 for more inspiration.

Furniture

BED

KING MATTRESS:
183 cm W × 203 cm D (6 × 6 ft 7 in)

QUEEN MATTRESS:
152 cm W × 203 cm D (4 ft 9 in × 6 ft 7 in)

DOUBLE MATTRESS:
135 cm W × 188 cm D (4 ft 4 in × 6 ft 2 in)

KING SINGLE:
105 cm W × 200 cm D (3 ft 4 in × 6 ft 6 in)

SINGLE BED:
90 cm W × 190 cm D (2 ft 9 in × 6 ft 2 in)

KING BEDHEAD:
190 cm W × 130–160 cm H
(6 ft 2 in × 4 ft 2 in – 5 ft 2 in)

QUEEN BEDHEAD:
160 cm W × 120–150 cm H (5 ft 2 in × 4–5 ft)

DOUBLE BEDHEAD:
145 cm W × 120–150 cm H (5 × 4–5 ft)

KING SINGLE BEDHEAD:
110 cm W × 105 cm H (4 × 3 ft)

SINGLE BEDHEAD:
90 cm W × 105 cm H (3 × 3 ft)

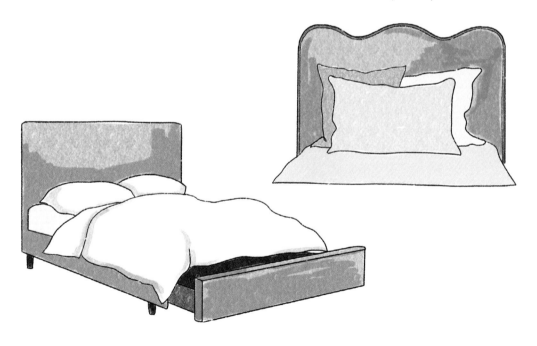

BEDSIDE TABLES

Bedside tables are meant to be practical pieces next to the bed for storing things you may need in the night. But they're also an excellent opportunity to jazz up your room. Your bedside tables will be the biggest indicator of your style after the bedhead. So choose wisely! Light oak timbers give off a coastal vibe whereas black with metal hardware can look more modern and contemporary.

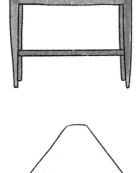

You'll want to make sure that your bedside table matches your mattress height. If it's too tall you'll struggle to get anything off it during the night. If it's too low, your bed covers will knock things off. Opt for a matching pair for symmetry.

SIZE GUIDE: 40–60 cm W × 50 cm D × 40–70 cm H (16–24 × 20 × 16–28 in)

BEDSIDE LIGHTS

Enhance the look of your room with some beautiful bedside table lamps. You can choose to make these a feature by opting for a bright colour or a striking stone base, or keep it simple with a stick base or reading arm-style light.

SIZE GUIDE: 60–80 cm H (24–31 in)

CHEST OF DRAWERS

These days most wardrobe storage is built in so there's not a lot of use for a chest of drawers. But if you're short on storage space it is an excellent additional storage solution for smaller pieces of clothing such as socks, underwear, bras, T-shirts and less frequently used clothing.

SIZE GUIDE: 80 cm W × 50 cm D × 78 cm H (31 × 20 × 31 in)

FLOOR LENGTH MIRROR

You'll need a full length mirror in your bedroom or walk-in robe to see your outfit as a whole. Whether it's extra large or just large enough to see most of your outfit will be determined by the amount of wall space that you have available.

SIZE GUIDE: 180 cm (71 in)

SCATTER CUSHIONS

No bed is ever truly finished until it has a few scatter cushions adorning it. But how many is too many and what sizes do you choose? Typically you have a mix of sizes for interest but you can keep it simple, too.

STYLING OPTION 1:
Two square cushions +
one lumbar cushion

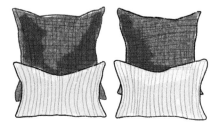

STYLING OPTION 2:
Two square cushions +
two lumbar cushions

STYLING OPTION 3:
Two lumbar cushions

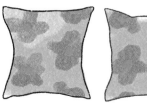

STYLING OPTION 4:
Two square cushions

WARDROBES

Planning your wardrobe is stressful. Thinking about where to house all your outfits, shoes, handbags and accessories takes a lot of brainpower and is often best left to the professionals. However, if you do want to design your wardrobe space there are some guidelines you should follow.

ASSESS WHAT YOU ALREADY OWN: Measure any items of clothing or shoes that are unusual lengths or heights that you may need to accommodate. Think about what you wear most and would want to access daily rather than occasionally. This is a great opportunity to throw away anything you have outgrown or no longer need, or that is beyond repair. Then you'll have a proper idea of how much you actually need to store.

GROUP LIKE WITH LIKE: Plan where you'll place T-shirts, pants, underwear, socks, dresses, shirts and so on. Do you want to have a summer section and a winter section, or will you have to rotate it with another wardrobe in the house?

YOUR PERSONAL PREFERENCES: Do you like to hang your T-shirts rather than fold them, or do you have a sneaker collection you want on display?

SHELVES AND DRAWERS VS HANGING SPACE: Do you want more drawer and shelf storage, or do you need to hang long dresses and coats? Plan your layout according to what you own and how you prefer to access the items.

FEATURES: Do you want a jewellery drawer built into your wardrobe with a lock so you can keep watches and jewellery safe? Maybe you want a special drawer for rolled up belts and ties. Perhaps you want a backlit mirror and dressing table for doing your make-up.

If you won't be looking at your wardrobe from the bed or as you walk through your room, you could ditch the doors and just have an open layout to keep costs down.

DESIGN CONSIDERATIONS

What do you do with the corners in U-shaped walk-in wardrobes? You can:

- put shoes on rotating turntables

- add wrap-around rods for hanging

- use corner shelves that wrap around.

The top shelves of your wardrobe are great for less commonly used items such as suitcases, winter bedding and hats.

LIGHTING

It's a good idea to add strip lighting underneath your wardrobe shelves as wardrobes can be dark, cavernous spaces where you lose a lot of items because you can't see them clearly.

CHOOSING COLOURS AND MATERIALS

You have different options for your wardrobe materials.

TWO-PAC FINISH: Special paint formulation to ensure longevity and durability

LAMINATE/MELAMINE: Imitate timber for a sophisticated look

SOLID TIMBER: Quality look that will last forever

MIRROR: Great solution for small rooms that need to appear larger while providing a full-length mirror.

CHOOSING HARDWARE

You've got three options when it comes to your door hardware.

KNOBS: Good for doors where all you have to do is pull the door open gently

HANDLES: Better for drawers so you can get your fingers into them and pull the drawers all the way out

FINGER PULL: Gives a seamless look because there's no distracting hardware.

WARDROBE LAYOUT

Don't forget to allow for short hanging, long hanging, shoe storage and drawers when planning your wardrobe layout.

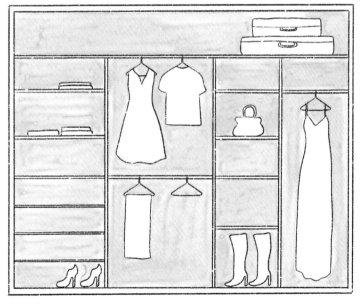

Floor plans

Your bed is the biggest piece of furniture in your bedroom, so it's vital that you place it in the best position possible. Once you've determined your bed placement, the other pieces of furniture all start to come together much more easily. The following illustrations offer some floor-plan ideas for you to try at home.

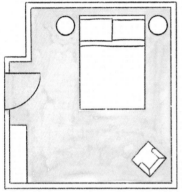

MASTER BEDROOM
WITH PARENTS' RETREAT

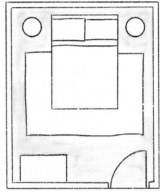

MASTER BEDROOM

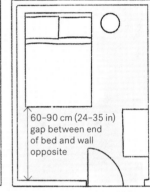

60–90 cm (24–35 in) gap between end of bed and wall opposite

SMALL BEDROOM

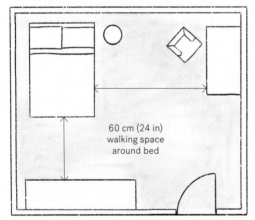

60 cm (24 in) walking space around bed

BEDROOM WITH DESK SPACE
(KID'S BEDROOM)

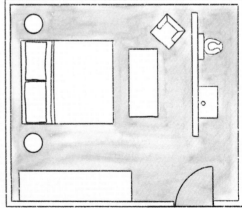

WARDROBE OR ENSUITE
BEHIND FLOATING WALL

Style Your Home

Styling guide

Beyond choosing practical pieces for your bedroom, it's important to add your own personality and twist to the decor. It's a great opportunity to create a comfortable and tranquil space that you really look forward to walking into each evening at bedtime.

STYLING THE BEDSIDE TABLE

There's an art to styling your bedside table. Putting too many items on the surface can be chaotic, while finding the balance of objects will make your room feel nice and cohesive. Of course, you can choose not to display anything at all and keep the bedside tables just for statement lamps, but if you want a few trinkets on display use the following guide.

Remember the triangle rule discussed earlier in the book? The same principle applies. Your lamp will be the tallest item so you'll need to work down from that point. Avoid using objects that are similar heights. You'll want to vary the height, size, shape and weight of the objects you place on your bedside table. Use dishes and bowls for low profile items.

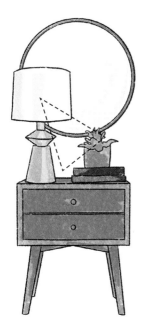

Items for bedside styling:

☐ Photo frame   ☐ Drink coaster

☐ Small plant   ☐ Water carafe

☐ Vase of flowers   ☐ Water glass

☐ Candle   ☐ Dishes

☐ Ring dish   ☐ Bowls

☐ Trinket tray

STYLING THE DRESSER

Do you want to display some treasured trinkets on your dresser or chest of drawers? You don't need to fill the top with items. You might need to keep it free for folding clothes or laying out the next day's outfit. This is where using a tray comes in handy. It corrals all of your items neatly and allows you to move the tray to the other side of the dresser if you need to create space.

Centre a mirror or a piece of art above the dresser to anchor it to the wall and to bounce more light into the room or inject some colour.

Items for your dresser:

☐ Tray

☐ Perfume bottles

☐ Books

☐ Diffuser

☐ Candle

☐ Lamp

☐ Potted orchid

☐ Potted plant

☐ Jewellery hanger

☐ Crystals

☐ Vases

☐ Dishes

☐ Objet d'art

☐ Photo frame

☐ Flowers

STYLING THE BED

You can get really lost in the bed-making process! Over-commit with too many cushions and you'll be making a rod for your own back each morning when you wake up and make the bed before heading out the door. Or under-commit and have your bed looking a little sad and uninviting.

Items to use to style your bed to perfection:

☐ Four standard pillows

☐ Two European pillows

☐ Fitted sheet

☐ Flat sheet

☐ Two pillowcases

☐ Two European pillowcases

☐ Quilt/doona cover

☐ Doona insert

☐ Throw rug

☐ Two square scatter cushions

☐ One lumbar cushion

No polyester or artificially made materials should be allowed on your bed. They may be a cheaper alternative but they will make you sweat too much at night because the material is not a breathable fabric like cotton or linen.

PLACING A RUG

Rugs are an excellent way to add proportions and scale to a room. A bed floating in the middle of the room without an anchor point underneath it can look a little lost or unfinished. By adding the right-sized rug under the bed you can completely transform your bedroom. It also gives you an opportunity to inject some colour or texture into the room.

Here's a diagram showing you the right way to add a rug to your room and the sizes to choose for each sized bed base so you're not second-guessing your purchases next time you go rug shopping.

KING BED RUGS:

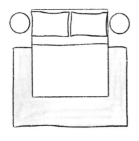 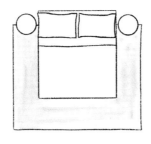 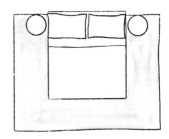

250 × 350 cm (8 × 11 ft)   300 × 400 cm (10 × 13 ft)   350 × 450 cm (11 × 15 ft)

QUEEN BED RUGS:

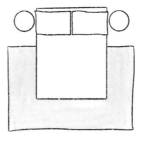 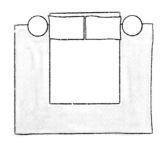

200 × 300 cm (7 × 10 ft)   250 × 350 cm (8 × 11 ft)

CHOOSING WINDOW TREATMENTS

reveal   frame

architrave

Depending on your budget, you can choose to layer your bedroom curtains and blinds or just opt for one solution. When deciding on your bedroom window treatments, you should take the following into consideration.

To reveal or not reveal? If you are really bothered by light when you sleep, you'll want to hang a roman blind inside the reveal or a roller blind on the outside of the reveal (with a back roll). These methods are the best ways to block the light that shines through either side of the blinds. This is especially helpful if you're a light sleeper who can't stand being woken up by sunlight or street lamps outside your window. If you only have curtains, hang your rod or rail overlapping the edge of the window so that light is blocked on the sides.

CURTAIN LENGTH OPTIONS

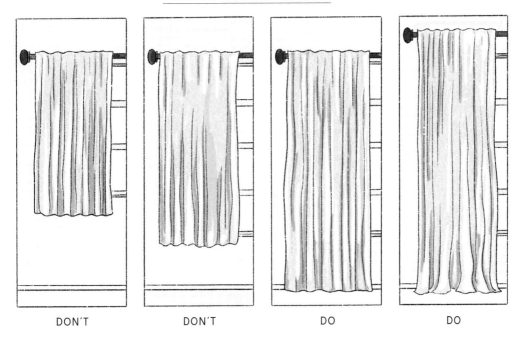

DON'T   DON'T   DO   DO

CONTROLLING LIGHT

You can use two window treatments in your bedroom to control the different light levels in the day. There are some great combinations to consider.

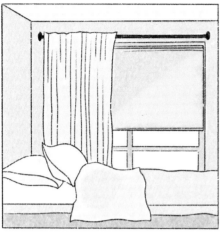

BLOCKOUT ROLLER BLINDS AT THE BACK,
SHEER CURTAINS AT THE FRONT

BLOCKOUT ROMAN BLINDS AT THE BACK,
SHEER CURTAINS AT THE FRONT

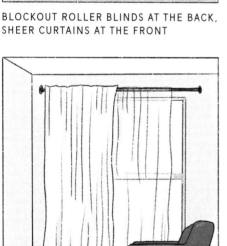

SHEER CURTAINS AT THE BACK,
BLOCK OUT CURTAINS AT THE FRONT

SHUTTERS AT THE BACK,
SHEER CURTAINS AT THE FRONT

Style Your Home

Fabric helps soften a room. If you have floorboards you'll need a fabric roman or curtain to help soften and warm up the space. As an added bonus it will help with sound absorption, so that when you walk through the room it won't echo so much.

To give you more privacy, use a double rod/rail to hang blockout curtains and sheers. If you want a more streamlined look, hang sheer curtains in front and a blockout backing on the rod behind rather than another textured fabric with a blockout backing. It's less bulky.

CHOOSING COLOURS

Choose complementary colours to your room palette or match to your wall colour. White can be harsh in a bedroom, so a flax linen or soft grey tones help soften the look and feel.

MOTORISING BEDROOM BLINDS AND CURTAINS

If you have really tall ceilings or a lot of windows in the room, you'll be standing there for ages trying to close them all manually with a pull cord. Motorisation is not a cheap option so budget for it in advance if you want to include it in your renovation, or it'll be the first thing you cut back on when you're trying to trim the budget down the track.

Troubleshooting

LACK OF SYMMETRY

The biggest no-no in feng shui is not having two bedside tables and two lamps either side of your bed. Why? Because according to feng shui principles, not having symmetry in the bedroom means your relationship (or lack of, if you only have one bedside table and lamp!) could be in jeopardy.

Having two of each promotes a harmonious relationship between the couple who share the bedroom. Or, if you're looking for love, it's showing that you have the space in your life for someone else to come in. The same goes for pushing the bed into one corner of the bedroom, because it stops someone else getting into the bed on the other side.

Outside of feng shui principles, it also just looks a lot better to have two of each on either side of the bed.

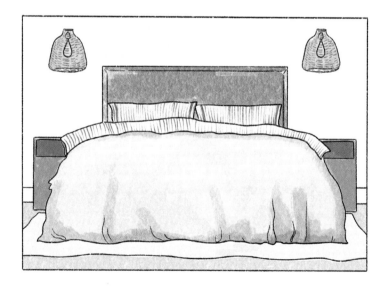

BED COVERS

Do you want to know how the professionals do it for magazine styling? Choose the next size up for your doona cover, coverlet or quilt to get that luxe hotel look. For example, if you have a queen bed, you'll want a king bed cover. For a king bed, opt for a super king bed cover.

A TV OR NOT?

This is a controversial one but if you truly want your bedroom to be for relaxation and a tranquil place to escape the world then hanging a huge TV on the wall opposite the bed is not ideal. Use the wall for a beautiful calm piece of art that helps you relax when you're drifting off to sleep each night.

BEDHEAD HEIGHT (OR NO BEDHEAD AT ALL!)

If you're placing your bedhead against a wall with a window on it you'll be a bit more limited in terms of the height you can go to, but generally you want it to sit at about 130–150 cm high (51–59 in). That way you'll see enough of the bedhead fabric above your pillows when they're stacked up on the bed.

If you have high ceilings, opt for a taller than average bedhead to give the room a bit more scale and proportion so it doesn't look like it is too short for the room. Also consider how high your mattress sits. If you've got a really deep mattress plus a pillow topper then you'll want a taller bedhead so that you can see more of it.

ADDING A MIRROR

If you typically get dressed in your bedroom, make sure you have a full-length mirror in the room so that you can see your entire outfit. Hang the mirror on the back of one of your wardrobe doors to keep it hidden from view when not in use. Or make a feature of it by opting for an ornately framed mirror that you can mount on the wall or lean against a wall.

RUGS ON CARPET – YES OR NO?

This is mostly just personal preference. The thickness of the rug plays a big part in whether or not you can put it on your carpet. Flatweaves work well as they're nice and thin but they do have a tendency to roll up at the edges, which looks messy and creates a tripping hazard. A tufted or hand-knotted wool rug that's nice and heavy in weight will sit solidly on your carpet without shifting around too much.

If you have a beautiful, tufted wall-to-wall carpet in your bedroom that's soft and luxurious to walk on, then there's probably no need to put a rug in the room as well.

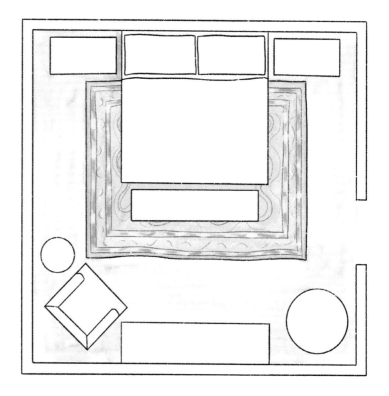

WORKING

The rise of working at home hit a peak in 2020 when the world turned upside down for a hot minute. Suddenly the dining table became a desk, homework station, and arts and crafts table. However, a space to work comfortably from home is not a new concept and a home office is often requested as part of a house design.

The work-from-home space is just as important as any other room, especially as it can be where people spend the majority of their day. So they need work surface space, a comfortable chair, appropriate height desk, and storage for books, paperwork, tech accessories and more.

How you choose to allocate your decorating and design budget to your home office largely depends on how often you'll use it and what your top priorities are. Generally, when designing space you need to pay a lot of attention to the desk, storage capabilities and backdrop behind you when you're on a video call. There's nothing more distracting than speaking to someone on screen and seeing the washing hanging behind them!

The home office doesn't have to be a fully dedicated room. If you're short on space, a small desk in another room that fits your needs is perfectly suitable. The same goes for built-in joinery. For example, your kitchen joinery could be extended to accommodate a desktop computer and some overhead storage. Everyone's work-from-home needs vary so the following information looks at a number of different possibilities.

Study hero

Purchasing a desk requires you to take a number of things into consideration, including dimensions, materials, ergonomics and style. However, don't let style rule your furniture purchase decisions. There are a number of considerations to think about.

PULL YOUR DESK CHAIR IN UNDER THE DESK: Chair arms hitting the edges of your desk and stopping you from sitting all the way under it is not only frustrating when you're trying to work, but will also scratch and wear away the finish of your desk.

LENGTH, DEPTH AND HEIGHT: Make sure these suit your needs. If you're building a desk into the wall of your home office this is much easier to manage as you can select the dimensions you want. Refer to the furniture list to check average depth and height dimensions.

ENOUGH STORAGE SPACE: Sometimes a desk will come with built-in drawers or shelves, but if these do not provide enough storage you'll need to plan bookshelves, floating shelves or built-in cabinetry to house the items you need to store.

CABLES AND CORDS: They're annoying but necessary so drill your own holes in your desk for cord storage or purchase a desk that already has pre-drilled holes for good cable management.

ASSEMBLE OR PRE-MADE: Most desks will come pre-made but check carefully before purchasing in case your desk turns up in pieces and you're left trying to screw all the legs together!

THINK ABOUT LONGEVITY: Who's using the desk and for what purpose? Maybe you have small children who want to use it for arts and crafts now, but eventually it will become a homework desk they use most nights.

INVEST IN GOOD MATERIALS: There's a tonne of different desk materials on the market, including laminates, glass/metal and solid wood. Ultimately your budget will probably influence what you purchase.

Furniture

DESK

This is the hero piece in the room and also the largest chunk of your home office budget.

SIZE GUIDE: 150–180 cm W × 60–75 cm D × 75 cm H
(59–71 × 24–30 × 30 in)

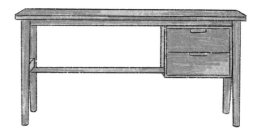

DESK CHAIR

Consider comfort levels as well as design aesthetics. Do you need wheels so you can move around the room easily or can you get away with purchasing an extra dining chair and using it as your study desk chair?

SIZE GUIDE: 45 W cm × 45 cm D × 80 cm H; seat height 45 cm
(18 × 18 × 31 in; seat height 18 in)

BOOKSHELVES

Not only are bookshelves a great place to house your book collection, they're also an opportunity to style and display some meaningful items in your home office, such as photo albums or a snow globe collected on a family holiday.

SIZE GUIDE: From 80 cm W × 30 cm D × 200 cm H
(31 × 12 × 79 in)

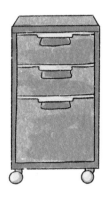

FILING CABINET

Filing cabinets are not so commonly used in home offices but they are useful if you need to store paperwork. They're not particularly attractive so if you can build it into some joinery or cabinetry you won't have to look at it all the time.

SIZE GUIDE: From 40 cm W × 50 cm D × 60 cm H
(15 × 20 × 24 in)

DESK LAMP

Lighting your work space well is a non-negotiable. Most task spaces require direct light like a desk lamp on an arm rather than a stick or straight base, so you can angle the lighting to the spot on the desk you need to see. Think about using a cool white light bulb as this will be the brightest option rather than a warm white bulb, which is a little less bright.

SIZE GUIDE: From 20 cm W × 15 cm D × 40 cm H
(8 × 6 × 16 in)

Floor plans

The home office can have more than one use, often doubling up as a guest room or sewing station. The following floor plans should help you to determine the best placement for your desk and any other important elements that need to be incorporated into the space.

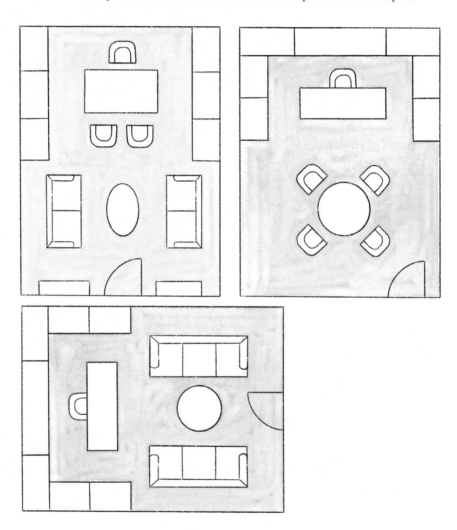

Styling guide

You don't want to clutter your workspace with all sorts of knick-knacks but it's nice to walk into your home office and feel that it shows your personality and interests.

STYLING YOUR DESK

A little tray on your desk housing some pretty things can jazz up a space where you sit to work for hours on end. There are many different items you can use.

- Photo frame
- Small plant
- Bud vase
- Diffuser

- Tray
- Drink coaster
- Water carafe
- Water glass

- Dishes
- Bowl

STYLING A BOOKCASE

When styling a bookcase you need to consider all the elements of styling,

BALANCE: You've got multiple flat shelves to work with. Decide if you want books on all the shelves or if you want to balance them out by placing the books off centre on some shelves or skipping sections of the shelf entirely.

SYMMETRY: Unless symmetry is important to you on your bookshelves, aim for asymmetrical placement of your styling items.

LIFE: Don't forget to add some life to your shelves. A beautiful pot with a cascading plant gives life and greenery to the space.

ANCHOR POINT: This can be hard to achieve because you're working with multiple flat surfaces rather than a single one such as the top of a sideboard. It's usually easier to choose the middle of the bookshelf as your anchor point, so place the largest grouping of books or largest solid object in the centre and style around it.

REPETITION: You have many shelves to work with, so use colours, textures and shapes in repetition across each shelf for consistency.

ODD GROUPINGS: Don't group things in even numbers. Opt for three to five items grouped together and don't just line them up in a row. You should use the full depth of the shelf.

VISUAL WEIGHT: Generally you should place the heaviest items at the bottom of your bookshelf and the lighter items at the top.

CHOOSING WINDOW TREATMENTS

You can often be in a home office for quite a long time, which means the light levels vary significantly throughout the day. If you're a night owl you'll be battling the dark, too!

Blinds, plantation shutters or curtains are all good options for your windows. Light control is important so you don't have sun in your eyes or glare on your screen, and can be seen easily on Zoom calls. Depending on where your windows face, think about installing two options so you have light control during the day as well as privacy if you face a busy street. If the home office also acts as a guest bedroom, you'll need blockout curtains or blinds for your guests at night.

Troubleshooting

STORAGE NEEDS

Built-in joinery is the best way to ensure that you are storing everything you need properly. Free-standing storage units or bookshelves are not always adequate for the paraphernalia that comes with most families and their home office needs.

Your needs will change over time so having built-in joinery means you have a variety of storage options. It also looks much more streamlined. You could even look at installing a wall bed to pull down when you need to house visiting guests.

PLACING YOUR DESK

In the world of feng shui, the placement of your desk is just as important as the placement of your bed and sofa. Place your desk in the centre of the room or pull it out from the wall. This means you can sit with your back against the wall rather than towards the door where you can't see surprise attacks coming!

ADDING DESIGN AND STYLE

A work space is a highly functional space, so sometimes the items you need for the room are not the most attractive. This applies particularly to sit-stand desks which, while ergonomically excellent, don't offer a lot of design interest.

You can counteract a very functional desk by using other flat surfaces as an opportunity to style and add some colour and fun into the room. Your bookshelves are a great place to show off your styling prowess and decorating skills!

Renovating the kitchen and bathroom

RENOVATING CREATES NURTURING SPACES,
ENHANCING DAILY RITUALS WITH LOVE.

A WORD ON RENOVATING

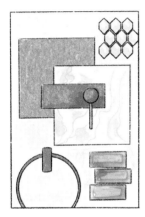

It's about time that can of worms was opened and all the important elements of your kitchen and bathroom renovations unpacked. These two rooms are the ones that cause the most amount of anxiety and sleepless nights because they're highly functional spaces, expensive to fit out and, once the fixtures are in, they're a lot harder and more expensive to swap out than the scatter cushions on your sofa. I know they were also the hardest rooms for me to design and commit to when I did my own renovation, which is ironic since I do it daily for clients. But even I struggled to make decisions and commit to tiles, splashbacks and colour palettes.

These chapters are full of practical advice to help make your decisions ten times easier. I'm often called on by clients to oversee their renovation projects so that they are not giving their contractor or builder the wrong dimensions or fixtures. It's the little things that can have a huge impact on the functionality of a space and, as a designer, I can spot these things on sight before they become a bigger issue to fix down the track. For example, my bathroom door used to swing into the shower screen, so when I renovated I asked the builder to re-hinge the door so that it swung away from the shower screen. It means I no longer hit the glass when I open the door, and it makes the room feel bigger and airier because the door opens flush against the wall instead of into the middle of the room.

The wet rooms of the house need to be installed by qualified tradespeople with plenty of experience. But there are still a lot of questions your trades or contractors will ask you when they're standing in your space deciding where the shower mixer will be hung or how high you want your toilet roll in the powder room. It's a good idea to educate yourself so that you don't slow down your renovation and can confidently make decisions on the spot. This will be your reference book for so many things when it comes to renovating your wet rooms. My hope is that it eases your renovating anxiety and helps you make really informed decisions about all of those nitty-gritty details.

Altering a physical space can bring up so many things for you. The upheaval of your worldly belongings, sorting through years of stored physical items with powerful memories attached to them, the dust, the decision fatigue, the budget constraints, the hidden costs that pop up, the time delays on products and the general disruption to your everyday life are not to be taken lightly.

If you're a believer in the power of feng shui, you'll know that the objects, placement and structure of your home (among other things) can have a profound effect on the humans who occupy that space. If you're interested in learning more about the placement of items within your home and how they can positively or adversely affect you, it would be wise to do some research into the art of feng shui.

Managing the stresses of money, time and space during a renovation can be challenging. A lack of planning will only amplify these demands. The aim of this section of the book is to give you a blue-print to follow through the process, so that when problems arise (and they will, trust me) you can be ready to minimise the impact, both financially and emotionally.

SO WHY RENOVATE?

There's a huge number of reasons why you decide to renovate.

- You love where you live and don't want to leave.

- The house has loads of potential.

- Council zoning will pass the plans you want to create.

- You have the means to do so (either money or the skill set to DIY).

- You want to keep your children settled in their neighbourhood and schools.

- Tired and broken fixtures need fixing in order to provide a more practical space to live in.

- It may be more cost-effective to renovate rather than buy something newer and move.

- You get exactly what you want when you renovate for yourself.

- You're close to work/play/city/ entertainment and moving might mean sacrificing some of these things.

- You can solve design dilemmas and inherent structural issues to create a happier space.

- You want to solve functional and style issues.

- You're using this house to get a better sale price so you can move to a larger home or level up your living quarters.

Lower your expectations during a renovation or lose them entirely. It's a temporary situation and you'll be back in your beautiful new space in no time. Yes, there'll be dust everywhere but it's nothing a bit of elbow grease can't solve once the renovation is over.

THE IMPORTANCE OF PLANNING

You could be living in your home for anywhere from five up to 20 years or more. If you're living in your forever home then you'll probably only renovate a handful of times, so you want to get it right. If you're renovating for profit in order to buy a larger home and keep working your way up the property ladder, then you'll be making the majority of your decisions guided by the return on investment.

Besides the purchase of your home, renovating is likely to be the largest chunk of money you'll spend in one hit so it needs to be worth it.

HIRED HELP

Who do you need on your team throughout a reno? There are many different professionals who are able to help with particular tasks along the way.

ARCHITECT: A trained professional who has the ability to design and construct buildings, with their services available from concept to completion. You would be wise to employ an architect to help design your home if you're wanting a very specific look, you're working with an older home and adding a very modern attachment, you have a difficult structure that needs a professional eye to help find the potential, or you possess no visualisation skills to see the potential of your home and need solid ideas to create wow factor.

DESIGNER: A designer can work in tandem with your architect to select hard and soft finishes for your home. From working out the best layout of your bathroom to picking tapware and solving design dilemmas, an interior designer will work closely with you throughout the project to ensure that the finished product is a beautiful harmony of function and form.

DECORATOR: A decorator typically works on the soft furnishings within your home, from furniture layout, window treatments for your windows, rugs and more. A decorator possesses the creative skills to walk into an empty space and picture the finished product filled with well-proportioned furniture that's practical and suits your needs while also looking beautiful and inviting.

PROJECT MANAGER: This is often split between a range of different trades or can be a specialist you hire to oversee the execution of your project. Often your builder will project manage as they are on site the most and can oversee each of the trades to ensure that it's all running smoothly. A project manager can manage things from fit-out timeframes and make decisions quickly so that the project keeps to time.

STRUCTURAL ENGINEER: Engineers provide a crucial role in your team of professionals to ensure that your structure is safe and secure. Not all projects require sign-off from a structural engineer, but the more difficult builds and tricky structures do.

BUILDER/CONTRACTOR: There are a number of different types of builders so you will need to decide which type is most suitable for your home build.

- **CUSTOM BUILDER:** Bespoke designs built exactly to your specifications. A great option for those wanting full control over the look of their home.

- **PROJECT BUILDER:** Pre-designed house and land packages for you to choose from. A cost-effective way to build a new home.

- **OWNER BUILDER:** You manage the entire project yourself and hire qualified trades to complete the work.

Hiring a designer

If you've recognised that you don't possess the necessary skills to make your home look and feel amazing then it's time to call in the help of a designer! A designer will manage and solve many problems.

DESIGNER VS DECORATOR

DESIGNER:

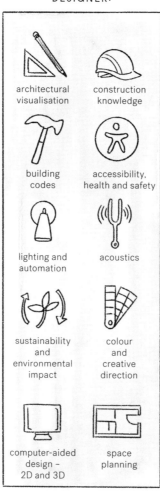

architectural visualisation

construction knowledge

building codes

accessibility, health and safety

lighting and automation

acoustics

sustainability and environmental impact

colour and creative direction

computer-aided design – 2D and 3D

space planning

DECORATOR:

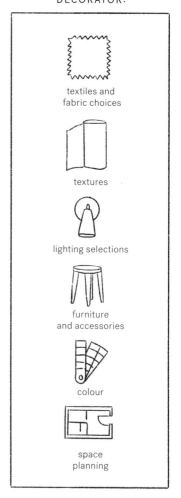

textiles and fabric choices

textures

lighting selections

furniture and accessories

colour

space planning

SAVES YOU TIME AND MONEY: Outsourcing to someone who already knows where to shop and what materials to avoid means you don't have to spend countless weekends at showrooms trying to figure out what tiles go with your taps.

SAVES YOUR MARRIAGE/RELATIONSHIP: If you've ever fought with your partner about sofa fabric choices, paint colours or how many cushions should be allowed on the bed, you'll know how helpful a third party is! Having a professional guide you through your choices can save a lot of deliberation time (that's code for arguing about kitchen tiles).

GIVES YOU ACCESS TO QUALITY TRADES: Designers have a whole list of trades and contractors they can recommend for jobs you don't have time to research and hire.

GIVES YOU ACCESS TO QUALITY PRODUCTS: Designers work with furniture wholesalers who won't sell to the general public.

GIVES YOU A FINISHED PRODUCT YOU'LL ABSOLUTELY LOVE: A designer's job at the end of the day is to create a beautiful, real and functional home for you (and your family) so that walking in the door each day makes you smile.

Committing to a designer is a bit like dating. You'll want to meet first to ensure that they're going to understand your brief clearly and then interpret it correctly to source products that you love.

Do the fit check first.

- Research their portfolio and service offering.

- Arrange a consultation with them so you can meet and decide if they feel like they can bring your thoughts to life.

- Do your homework. Research styles and trends so you can clearly articulate or show your designer what you're trying to achieve. They're not mind readers and a picture paints a thousand words so visuals always help!

How it works

- **INITIAL CONSULT:** This is the first chance to meet with your designer or decorator and get a feel for whether or not they're the right person for your project. Your designer will ask questions, listen to your biggest design dilemmas, make initial suggestions for design alterations, map an idea of traffic flow through the room, discuss colours, designs and patterns with you in detail, and try to determine your goals. It is typical for designers to charge for this initial consultation.

- **SCOPE OF WORKS:** After meeting with you, your designer will send you a proposal document, also known as a scope of works, that outlines the scope of each area you discussed together. Each designer determines their rates differently from pricing by the hour to package rates. This will all be explained in your scope of work. This is usually accompanied by a contract and first deposit instalment invoice.

- **CONCEPT CREATION:** This is the very first stage in the design process, where your designer or decorator will hash out the overall look and feel of your project before diving into the technical details. They will create a PDF document showing you ideal outcomes, inspirational images, colour palette ideas and floor-plan layouts for your feedback before moving to the next phase.

- **DESIGN DEVELOPMENT:** Stage two involves the decorator picking out all the detailed elements to bring your rooms to life, from rugs, table lamps and art to upholstered items. It's then typically presented to you as a mood board, either digitally or physically, with small sample swatches of fabrics, rugs, wallpapers and other textures.

- **JOINERY DRAWINGS:** If you require your designer to design custom joinery for you, stage three is when they start drawing up your joinery concepts for you to review and give feedback. It's all drawn to scale so that you can get a feel for the storage, wardrobes and TV units required for your home. Your drawings are usually presented to you in PDF form.

- **FURNITURE, FITTINGS AND EQUIPMENT (FF&E):** Stage four, also known as the Project Bible, is the detailed spreadsheet document for your trades to follow throughout the project. It details every single thing they need to know about the items you've chosen for your home and where they go.

- **FURNITURE SOURCING:** Once the build is well and truly underway, your designer moves to stage five and finds all the beautiful furniture pieces to finish off the new spaces and do them justice.

- **INSTALL AND STYLING:** A service offered by most designers and decorators is styling your home once all the items have been delivered, so that the house looks like the images created through the design process. At this stage you can sit back, relax and enjoy your beautiful new home!

PROJECT MANAGEMENT

Project management is a massive part of the process. If you are not confident doing this yourself, or you live too far away from the site to oversee decisions, you'll want to outsource this task to a professional.

Having the right people on your renovation team will minimise mistakes and prevent headaches you'd otherwise have to deal with alone.

Some tips for project managing

- Detail everything for your trades in a spreadsheet usually referred to as the FF&E Schedule.

- Order all your prime cost items (PC items) well in advance so that when your trades are ready, there are no delays because of product supply issues.

- Store them at your suppliers' warehouses or in your/friend/ family member's garage until you need them.

- Be on site often, and take photos and notes to discuss with your trades if they are not on site when you're there.

- Ask trades for their build schedule so you know what's happening at key milestones and what days you'll likely to be required on site for decision-making.

- You want to be on site for the following milestones at the very least:

  - PLUMBING ROUGH IN: This is when you decide where the taps will be located, discuss any issues they've found from demolition that need addressing, toilet placement etc.

  - ELECTRICAL ROUGH IN: This is when you choose where your light switches, power points, exhaust fan, heated towel rail and underfloor heating panels are put. You should also discuss if your switchboard needs upgrading or replacing. This is a great opportunity to add extra power points or better lighting.

  - PLUMBING FIT OFF: This is when the plumber comes back to install your tapware and connects all your water pipes. You'll want to be on site to determine where vanity-mounted mixer taps and the kitchen sink tap go in case they need to cut the stone top for the tap to be mounted, as well as other things such as the height of the toilet-roll holder, and placement of the hand-towel holder.

  - TILE SET OUT: This is important if you have chosen a tile configuration that is unique or your room has a difficult layout that requires you to be there in person to see the layout come together. You'll need to discuss where tiles need to be cut, what metal trims or mitred edges you want, where tiles meet other surfaces such as floorboards or door skirting boards and so on. You'll also need to discuss specific issues; for example, thick tiles stopping you from having flush-mounted power points that stick out too far from the wall and become an eyesore.

All of the above can sound scary and overwhelming but this is why it's important to hire the right people to help you as they'll be the ones to guide you and educate you throughout the process. Ask as many questions as you want to alleviate any of your concerns or worries. That's what you're paying for and what they're there for!

RENOVATING
THE KITCHEN

Surely the hardest working room in the house, kitchens are where the magic happens. Connections are made between family members and guests, and fond memories are formed. Many people hold lovely memories of sitting on the kitchen counter with a grandmother baking something wonderful. Or sneaking a taste of the cake batter when Mum turned her back.

Kitchens represent comfort, warmth, creativity and personal expression in the creation of all sorts of delicious and experimental dishes – some that never get repeated and others that become regular family favourites.

Cooking and preparing a delicious meal for your loved ones or guests is one of the strongest ways to show your love. So it comes as no surprise that planning a kitchen layout and the colours, textures and practicality are some of the most stressful parts of a renovation or new build because of the fear of getting it wrong and messing with those important life moments. Kitchen design is the most commonly outsourced part of the renovation process.

There is so much that goes into designing a kitchen and it is an extremely personal process. Many people make the mistake of designing a kitchen for resale, and while that may make sense to you at the time, it doesn't serve you – the one who's spending the money and using the space – at all. It's making assumptions about how strangers you haven't met will use the space. Where's the passion and thought in that? The next owner might rip the kitchen out the minute they move in because it doesn't work for their family unit. Design the kitchen for you and make the choices for your family's happiness. Obviously there are some choices that can make it more universally acceptable but ultimately you're the one spending your hard-earned money, time and effort.

So how do you do this? There are so many ways you can design a kitchen to suit specific needs. The first thing to do is to write a list of *must-haves* and *nice-to-haves*. This will help determine whether you start the process with an interior designer, a specialised kitchen designer or do it yourself.

Must-haves vs nice-to-haves

These differ greatly from house to house and person to person. Here are some examples.

$ = INEXPENSIVE ADDITION

$$ = MODERATE ADDITION

$$$ = COSTLY ADDITION

Walk-in pantry – $$$

Integrated appliances – $

Task lighting – $

Wine fridge – $$

Coffee machine – $

Recycling and adequate rubbish bins – $

Statement splashback – $$$

Smart appliances – $$

Soft-close cabinetry – $

Pull-out drawers – $

Decorative hardware – $$

Decorative door profiles – $$

Stone benchtops – $$

Drawers vs doors – $$

Appliance storage – $$

Small appliance station (toaster, kettle, etc) – $$

Double oven – $$

Free-standing oven – $

Gas or induction cooktops – $

Integrated rangehood – $$

Gooseneck taps – $

Boiling water tap – $$

Feature island pendant lighting – $$

Pot filler tap – $$

Double bowl sink – $

Kitchen layouts

There are myriad options for kitchen layouts, some more functional than others. The following layouts are those most commonly used.

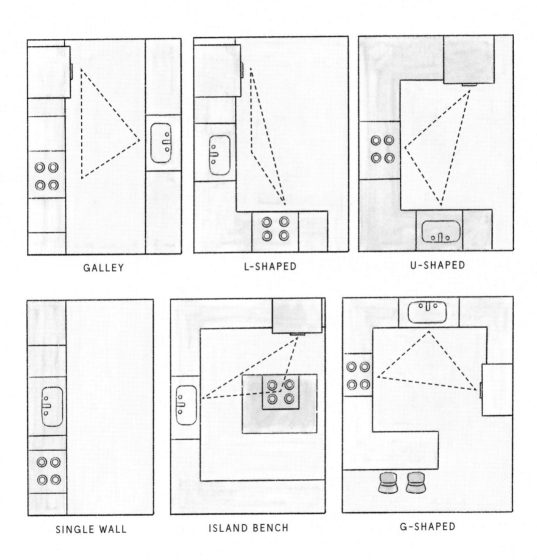

GALLEY

L-SHAPED

U-SHAPED

SINGLE WALL

ISLAND BENCH

G-SHAPED

HOW TO DETERMINE ISLAND PLACEMENT

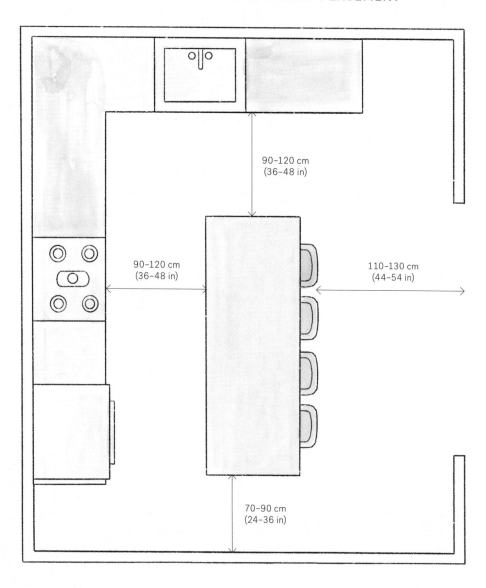

90-120 cm
(36-48 in)

90-120 cm
(36-48 in)

110-130 cm
(44-54 in)

70-90 cm
(24-36 in)

Determining style

This is the very first decision you should be making when it comes to designing your kitchen. As mentioned earlier, the architecture of your home, the era or decade your house was built in and the environment in which you live are all indictators of your style. So first up, decide if you're opting for an uber-modern kitchen or a more classic and traditional design.

CREATING A COHESIVE DESIGN

You need to choose a lot of different materials from different suppliers when designing your kitchen, from your flooring choice to your cabinetry, benchtop, splashback, appliances and tapware. So how do you know if it's all going to look okay? There can be a lot of decision fatigue or even analysis paralysis. You can be too scared to commit to one material knowing there's a knock-on effect for each decision.

There's no need to be scared. Following these steps will give you boundaries and guidelines when making decisions and bring together a cohesive kitchen design.

Your key areas are the benchtop, splashback, cabinetry and, of course, appliances. It would be wise to grab colour swatches for each of them to keep on hand throughout the design process so that you can be sure they all work well together.

CHOOSING A BENCHTOP

You are spoilt for choice when it comes to what is available. Here's a look at the most popular options.

NATURAL STONE: Granite and marble offer durability and heat resistance. They have a lovely tactile surface that adds a classy, elegant touch to your kitchen. Marble can be a fickle material as it's porous and requires a bit of maintenance, so that it isn't stained or scratched easily. Natural stone is a perfect choice for both modern and classic kitchen spaces. Your choice of benchtop profile will dictate if you have a classic or modern look.

ENGINEERED STONE: Made to emulate natural stone but less high maintenance. There are so many varieties on the market from a huge range of brands, so there's generally a colour or texture to suit everyone. Since engineered stone looks a lot like natural stone, you can get away with using it in both modern and classic styles.

SOLID SURFACE: Materials such as Corian are a fantastic choice for people wanting a really customised look with curved benchtops or unique designs. It is extremely versatile with the great advantage of being repairable. Any chips can be easily filled and sanded back to make the chip virtually undetectable. Generally only used in modern-looking kitchens.

LAMINATE: A budget-friendly option that is super easy to clean and comes in a huge range of colours and patterns that mimic marble and a natural stone look. Laminates are generally used in a modern-looking kitchen.

TIMBER: Not the ideal surface material for a benchtop because kitchens are wet areas, but it does provide a nice rustic look. Just don't forget to seal it often to keep it looking good.

CONCRETE: Another fabulous kitchen benchtop option that looks nice and streamlined in terms of colour. Just be sure to seal it regularly as it can be a porous surface. Concrete gives an edgy, modern look to your kitchen.

METALS: Stainless steel and zinc are less popular choices but offer durability and add an industrial look and feel to your kitchen, making them a great choice for warehouse conversions.

CHOOSING A BENCHTOP PROFILE

Your choice of benchtop profile (also known as the edge profile and thickness of your benchtop) is a big design dictator. Your choice of profile will determine many other design decisions in the kitchen so choose carefully!

Below is a list of different profiles and their styles.

MODERN STYLES:

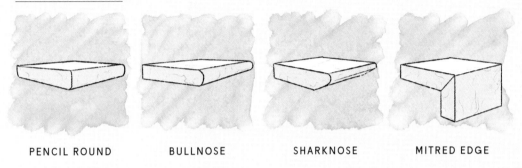

PENCIL ROUND   BULLNOSE   SHARKNOSE   MITRED EDGE

CLASSIC STYLES:

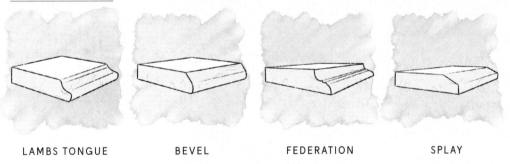

LAMBS TONGUE   BEVEL   FEDERATION   SPLAY

CHOOSING A SPLASHBACK

TILES: The most commonly chosen splashback option as they allow you to have a feature or focal point in the kitchen. Tile trends date quite quickly, however, so opt for something a bit more timeless, such as a subway or marble mosaic to ensure that your kitchen looks great for years to come.

STONE/ENGINEERED STONE: A great choice for that streamlined look with the benchtop continuing up the wall. Just be mindful that your cooktop will need enough clearance so that it doesn't damage the stone behind it. Streamlining your benchtop with your splashback gives a bit more of a modern edge to the room. This is especially useful if you've got a small space you need to make appear larger.

MIRRORS/WINDOWS: If you're short on natural light, a great way to inject some light into your kitchen is to turn your splashback into a long narrow window. Alternatively, under-cabinet lighting with a mirrored splashback means you get a lot more light added to your room for very little effort. Choose an antique-mirrored finish for a more traditional look.

CHOOSING CABINETRY

Your choices of benchtop and splashback will dictate a certain look and feel for your kitchen, but the door profiles and colours you choose for your cabinetry will be a real marker of time and trends.

LAMINATE OR MELAMINE: Gives you a wood look but it's constructed from thin-pressed wood board with a printed image of wood fused onto it, making it a more affordable option in a huge range of colours.

TIMBER VENEER: A thinly sliced layer of real timber applied to MDF or particle board gives the look of solid wood without the price tag.

TWO-PAC FINISH: Allows you to have almost any colour you like for your kitchen cabinets as paint is tinted to the colour you like and sprayed on the doors. It's a hard-wearing choice that gives you an alternative to timber.

SOLID TIMBER: Certainly a more luxurious-looking option for your kitchen but it does come with a price tag.

DOOR PROFILES

The profile you choose will be the most obvious indicator of the style and design era you are aiming for.

FLAT PROFILE:
Conscious of budget? A flat door is the most cost effective as it's got no decorative profile feature. You can jazz it up with a door handle or keep it plain and have it as a finger pull door for a streamlined look.

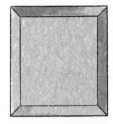

BEVELLED PROFILE:
The bevelled edging is a sophisticated yet simple option.

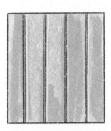

V-GROOVE PROFILE:
Offers a great option for a modern country look.

SHAKER PROFILE:
Gives off a very Hamptons classic look.

GLASS PROFILE:
If you want to show off certain things like nice glassware or dinnerware, opting for glass-fronted doors allows you to do this. You can frost the glass or leave it as is depending on what kind of look you're after.

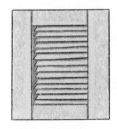

LOUVERED PROFILE:
This gives a very coastal feel. Great for beachside homes wanting a different look.

REEDED PROFILE:
Grooves are rounded out, giving a lovely decorative door profile.

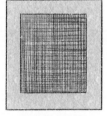

MESH PROFILE:
Think about adding some brass or steel mesh inserts into your door panels to really elevate the look of your kitchen.

SLIM PROFILE:
This modernised look has a smaller profile around the edges.

FLUTED PROFILE:
The opposite to reeded, a fluted profile has grooves cut into the panel to give it interest.

CHOOSING APPLIANCES

You need quite a few electrical appliances in a kitchen so the thought required prior to purchasing is important. Some of your appliances will be used together so ease of access to each is a factor to consider. For example, you can't be opening your dishwasher into the same space you'd be opening an oven door or it will create chaos when you're busy cooking a big meal.

There are a number of key considerations when it comes to choosing appliances.

BUDGET

Having a clear idea of what you want to spend is very important. It will help you narrow down which brands you should be looking at when you first visit an appliance showroom or start researching online.

STYLE

Choosing between a modern or classic look means you can narrow down the brands quite quickly, as some specialise in modern while others do classic looks really well.

SIZE

If you have a difficult layout or very specific size requirements, working out the maximum width, depth and height of your appliances will help narrow down your choices very quickly. For example, if you can only fit a really narrow dishwasher (450 mm wide; 18 in), you'll quickly work out there are only a handful of brands that sell that size, which makes your choice easier!

FEATURES

Have you got your heart set on certain features such as a fridge door with an ice machine, a steam oven or a wifi-controlled rangehood? Make a wishlist of fancy features you'd really love and instantly rule out the brands that don't meet your requirements.

LONGEVITY

Buy once, buy well. You don't want to be replacing appliances often. It gets expensive very quickly and also introduces a range of other issues such as retrofitting a new oven into an old oven's spot. It rarely ends well. Buying the best quality you can afford at the time is the way to go.

SERVICEABILITY

There are no laws saying you should choose all your appliances from the same brand but it certainly makes it a lot easier to get them serviced if you only need to rely on one service provider. Research the brand prior to committing and read reviews on warranty issues and customer experiences.

AVAILABILITY

Working to a quick turnaround? If so, your design decisions will largely be dictated by what's in stock when you go shopping! This is why it's best to plan ahead as much as possible. It's very disappointing to fall in love with the perfect oven only to find out it's got a 14-month lead time and you need it installed in seven weeks.

Keep in mind that some appliances can be slightly deeper than your cabinetry. If that's the case you can build out your cabinetry a few millimetres (or inches) to accommodate and then your cabinetry all lines up nicely with your appliances. This is particularly important if you're opting for integrated appliances such as dishwashers.

CHOOSING TAPWARE

Most homes will have the same coloured metal throughout the house, so door knobs, cabinet handles, and kitchen and bathroom taps will all be the same metal. You can certainly mix it up and choose different colour options but it does give a more elevated look when they match.

This means that if your tap is brass, your door handles, lighting and cabinet handles are all brass for consistency and cohesiveness.

WINDOW TREATMENTS FOR YOUR KITCHEN

There are a number of options for window coverings in your kitchen.

PLANTATION SHUTTERS: A great solution for maintaining privacy as well as filtering light. They have the added bonus of being durable enough to wipe clean if any cooking oil or splatters make their way onto the shutter blades. However, note that shutters open out in a really large footprint so be mindful of anything that hangs or sits in the way.

ROMANS: Fabric is a risk in a kitchen as it's very absorbent (think cooking smells and spills) but it does soften all harsh and cold textures and is a great way to add pattern and colour.

ROLLERS: While easy to wipe clean, they are less attractive to look at when compared to shutters or romans.

CAFE CURTAINS: These are a cute concept, sitting halfway across the window instead of hanging the full length. Think Parisian bakery window!

FULL-LENGTH CURTAINS: These are only advisable if you have a really large kitchen with an eat-in space away from cooking oils and spills, with floor-to-ceiling windows or a bay window.

ROMANS

CAFE CURTAINS

Hanging an island pendant

Generally you'll have an island pendant either above your kitchen bench or your dining table in an open-plan space (see page 120). Too many feature lights in a small space will overpower the room. If you need additional lighting for task lighting then it's best to light up your island bench. If you're only adding them for decorative reasons then hanging a beautiful pendant above your dining table is a great way to make a striking feature. Don't forget that if you were to move your dining table, the pendant would be too low so only commit if you know that's where the table will stay.

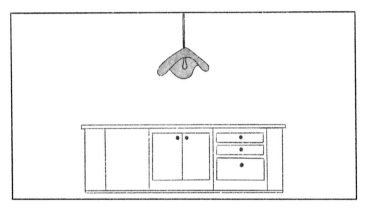

SINGLE PENDANT

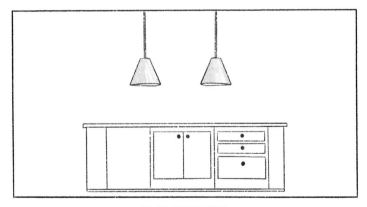

TWO PENDANTS

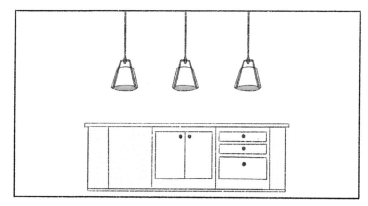

THREE PENDANTS

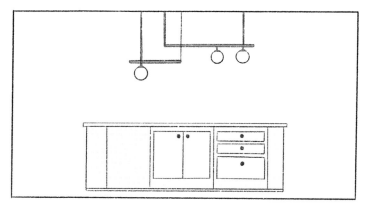

LINEAR/BAR PENDANT

Door profiles

You can mix and match the types of door profiles you have in your kitchen. For example, you can have a reeded door profile for your island bench with flat doors for the remaining cabinetry. This not only keeps costs down but also gives the room interest and allows the island bench to be the hero focal point.

Choosing cabinetry

Map the functionality of your kitchen cabinetry well in advance. Think long and hard about the items you actually need to store. Drawers are much more functional than doors when it comes to kitchen design. They allow you to have a bird's eye view, whereas doors and shelves mean that you lose things at the back of the cabinet really easily.

Also consider making all shelves adjustable to give you flexibility for storing large items. You'd hate to go to all the effort of designing your kitchen only to realise your KitchenAid mixer doesn't fit into any of the cabinets. The added benefit of drawers is that they're a bit harder for small children to get into so it keeps the kitchen a little bit more kid-proof!

While we're on this topic, think about handles vs no handles for your doors and drawers.

To integrate or not integrate

Integrating your dishwasher or fridge is a lovely way to get cohesion with your kitchen cabinetry and hides away or disguises otherwise unattractive appliances. This is especially important if you have a specific colour palette you're sticking to and don't want a big stainless steel or black appliance pulling focus. Let's face it, you rarely want your appliances to be the focal point, unless of course it's a big beautiful free-standing oven that sits front and centre in your kitchen.

So, when would you not install an integrated appliance?

BUDGET CONSTRAINTS: They're more expensive than regular appliances and you also need your cabinet maker to construct a false door for the appliance.

MAINTENANCE: Because the door is fixed to your kitchen cabinetry it can make maintenance a little tricker as there's an added layer to consider when fixing a broken machine.

EASE OF USE: Buttons for an integrated dishwasher are inside the door so if it bothers you that you can't see how long is left until the load is complete then integrating might be an issue.

Cabinetry to the ceiling?

If you have high ceilings, don't go for a standard height upper cabinets or it'll make the room feel shorter. Make the most of your wall height by carrying your upper cabinets to the ceiling. This not only gives you more storage space, it'll make the room feel taller and more elegant.

Applying the colour rule

Refer back to the Contrast section (see page 45) detailing the colour formula 60/30/10. The same colour rule is applied to kitchens.

PRIMARY COLOUR: This doesn't just have to be your kitchen cabinets. You may want a Calacatta marble benchtop and matching splashback. This would mean that your primary colour is the marble veining. Or you could opt for navy cabinetry, which would mean that the primary colour for your kitchen is navy because it's the dominant colour.

SECONDARY COLOUR: This is typically your stone elements or tiles, but if you don't have a massive amount of cabinetry in your kitchen (like a small galley kitchen) then your cabinet colour may be your secondary colour.

ACCENTED WOW FACTOR: This could be the kitchen floor, kitchen splashback or even just small timber accents such as open floating shelves in an oak timber. It could also be the benchtop appliances you choose, such as a powder blue KitchenAid mixer or matching yellow toaster and kettle set. It doesn't always have to be the hard finishes that make up your accented colour.

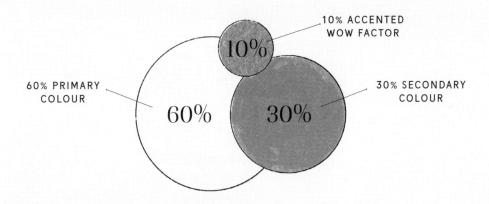

60% PRIMARY
COLOUR

10% ACCENTED
WOW FACTOR

30% SECONDARY
COLOUR

60%

10%

30%

RENOVATING
THE BATHROOM

Bathrooms are usually thought of in terms of cleanliness and personal hygiene, yet they also provide you with a private sanctuary where you can unwind, de-stress and rejuvenate. They can become a sanctuary where you can escape and relax without any interruptions (so long as you install a lock so no little people can pay you a visit while you're trying to soak in the tub!). Think of the times you've stayed in a beautiful hotel or visited a day spa and spent longer than normal in the beautiful surroundings and taking in the quiet moments. That's the feeling you want when planning your own bathroom.

There are so many elements to keep in mind for your bathroom design because ultimately it needs to be an uber-practical place that can withstand heavy-duty use. However, that doesn't mean the room has to look boring or uninviting.

Incorporating functionality and beauty in a bathroom is a challenge. You need to plan for the fact that anything and everything might get wet, whether you intend it to or not. You need to consider the impact of daily steam and the possibility of mould. You also need to plan the layout carefully, from the placement of the shower, drains, toilet, bath, vanity, towel rails and more. If you're renovating an existing space, you'll have certain challenges such as sewer pipes, plumbing and electrical connections to work around. Sometimes that makes things easier as it takes away a layer of decision-making when you know you can only have the toilet in one position. But that's only if the previous owners had positioned it in the right spot to start with.

Your bathroom is definitely not a room you can tackle on your own. Most people will employ the services of qualified tradespeople for their bathroom fit-outs. However, there is no harm in educating yourself in standard measurements and terminology when picking out your finishes and fixtures.

Lean on your trades as much as you want when completing a bathroom fit-out. They do it day in and day out and have a great wealth of knowledge. They have also likely been exposed to many different designs and installations, so if you're working with an unusual design you'll be guided by them.

Planning a bathroom renovation (or from scratch for a new build) requires a pretty serious level of planning before you can start doing any work. A bathroom is used multiple times a day for different tasks, so a great deal of thought needs to be put into the functionality as well as the beautiful fixtures. But there's no reason why your bathroom can't be beautiful and functional.

It's likely that you'll need almost every trade to work on your bathroom and they'll need to return to the site a couple of times to see the job through.

The bathroom team

PLUMBER: This is an obvious one but still worth mentioning! Your plumber will install water pipes, replace or relocate fixtures, and work on sewer pipes and stormwater drains if needed.

ELECTRICIAN: The electrician will wire up all your light switches, underfloor heating, powerpoints, exhaust fans and placement of overhead and wall lights.

WATERPROOFERS: This is an essential part of the process. Your waterproofers will apply a waterproof membrane to all wet areas (walls and floors) to prevent any leaks and damage to your home.

RENDERERS: If you have brick walls you'll probably need a renderer to come in and lay screed over the walls before the tiler or painter can get to work.

TILER: It always pays to invest in a really good tiler as a bad tile job can look horrendous and cost a fortune to fix if it's not been done properly the first time.

CARPENTER: The carpenter will make any structural changes to the room, framing up walls and hanging doors.

JOINER: The joiner is responsible or any custom timber joinery such as a vanity.

GLAZIER: The glazier will install shower screens or mirrors.

PAINTER: The painter will paint the walls and ceiling and is one of the last trades to be brought in.

SPECIALTY TRADES: If you're aiming for a more bespoke bathroom, you might also be engaging trades such as venetian plasterers, wallpaperer, or shutter and blind installers for window treatments.

What's the process?

Having a structured plan in place before starting to renovate is vital to the overall success of your bathroom renovation. The following steps take you through the process from start to finish.

- **PLANNING THE BATHROOM:** Either with a designer or on your own, map out what fixtures you want where, what walls might need to be moved, what additional services you need to add (for example, a powerpoint in the shaving cabinet or allowing for underfloor heating). Now is also when you'd want to be engaging a builder/contractor to get a price for their services so you can create a budget to work to.

- **SELECTION OF FIXTURES AND FITTINGS:** Once you've mapped out your layout, it's time to start selecting the specific pieces you want. Your builder or contractor will require all of these items to be selected and purchased prior to starting work so if you are not confident doing this yourself in showrooms or online, now is the time to enlist the help of a designer to help select all the items required for a seamless look.

- **DEMO:** The first day of the renovations has officially begun! This is a noisy and very dusty day as everything is removed from the existing bathroom to make way for the new.

- **PLUMBING ROUGH IN:** Once the demo is complete or the framing is up for the new bathroom, the plumber gets to work mapping out where all of your taps and sewer pipes will be placed. All of this needs to happen well before your tiler starts so that any pipes can be moved across the floor or walls to suit the new layouts.

- **ELECTRICAL ROUGH IN:** The electrician will map out where you need light switches, underfloor heating display screens, heated towel rails and powerpoints.

- **WATERPROOFING:** Once the services are in place you'll need to have the floors and walls waterproofed before the tiler can start work. If you're installing underfloor heating you'll need two waterproofing sessions.

- **UNDERFLOOR HEATING/SCREED:** If you're installing underfloor heating you'll need to have this installed before tiling. Then a layer of screed is required over the top of the underfloor heating so that you can waterproof over the top of this before tiling.

- **TILING:** This is an important day and you'll probably want to be on site. The tiler will need to know where you want the tiles laid, what grout colour you want, any specific tile lay patterns and any other details that will make or break the design of the room.

- **FIT OFF:** This is when your plumber and electrician return to site to install your tapware, power-point switches and light switches so they all function nicely!

Focal point

Your first step is to plan where everything goes. If you're working with an existing space, you'll need to determine if you have enough floor space or if you need to move walls. Next you'll need to determine if your services can remain in the same space or need to be moved to a different area of the room. Moving can be costly so keeping your plumbing and electrical connections in their original positions is a great budget saving tip.

Stand in the doorway of your bathroom to see the room as a whole. Think about where you want the focal point of the bathroom to be. It could be your vanity and mirror or a shower with a really decorative tile or a full feature wall with a gorgeous bath mounted underneath. The toilet is usually not on full display as you walk in the door. Generally it is tucked behind another element in the room to provide a bit more privacy and to hide what is something of an eyesore. Whatever your focal point, plan it in advance so that the rest of the room can fall into place from there, and make sure it's literally front and centre so it's easy to see from the second you walk into the room.

Tiles

Picking your tiles can be overwhelming. Even the professionals sometimes struggle to put different tile combinations together. There are a tonne of decisions to make so here is the process broken down to make it easier for you:

First you need to determine the types of tiles you want to use.

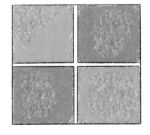

CERAMIC: Made in a kiln, ceramic tiles are baked at high temperatures to remove all moisture from them, which results in a hard-wearing tile.

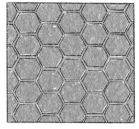

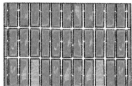

PORCELAIN: The most durable and less porous tile option, which is suitable for all bathrooms and perfect for floors and walls.

MOSAICS: Very small tiles usually used in bathrooms or as kitchen splashbacks. They come pre-mounted on mesh and are usually sold by the sheet (300 × 300 mm; 12 × 12 in).

SLABS: Large format tiles used for more impact in bathroom design.

TERRACOTTA: Clay ceramic tiles in mostly deep orange or red tones. Great for an earthy look.

ENCAUSTIC: Ceramic tiles where clay is inlaid in specific patterns and colours and fired at high temperatures.

A feature wall or floor can enhance the look of your bathroom beautifully, but if you're worried about it dating faster than tiling, here are some tips to help you.

FEATURE WALLS

You've got a couple of options for feature walls: behind the bath or down one long wall of the bathroom. Whether the feature is in the pattern, the colour or the way you lay the tiles on the wall, there's a whole range of different ways to make a feature wall.

FEATURE FLOORS

Feature floors really only work well if you have a large expanse of space in the room. If it's a relatively small bathroom that has a lot of fixtures on the floor then it probably wouldn't work to have a fussy feature floor. If you choose to do a feature floor, keep your wall tiles a little simpler.

FEATURE NOOK

Think about tiling your shower niche with a feature tile that complements the other bathroom tiles to make a little feature within your shower. Details like that really give off a luxe look.

TILE LAYOUT

Once you've made the important design decisions about the colour and pattern of your tiles, you have to consider layout. The following examples give you some options to consider.

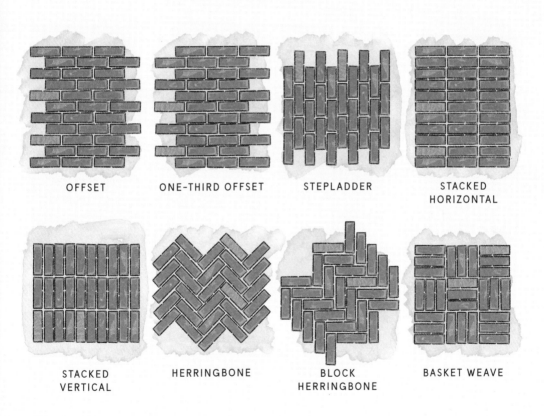

OFFSET   ONE-THIRD OFFSET   STEPLADDER   STACKED HORIZONTAL

STACKED VERTICAL   HERRINGBONE   BLOCK HERRINGBONE   BASKET WEAVE

TILE HEIGHT

You have a couple of options when choosing bathroom tile heights. You don't always have to tile to the ceiling.

Full height is great for making shorter ceilings look taller, as it draws your eye upwards. This is the most common choice for homeowners as it means that the walls stay protected.

Tiles at three-quarter height are more typically seen in older style homes such as those built during the Victorian and Art Deco eras. It's also a great way to save on tiles and labour as you are not tiling the top quarter of the room.

Chair rail, or dado rail, is about the halfway mark on the wall. You wouldn't do this for a shower as you need to tile the entire shower, but it's a great line to tile to before switching to a different style of tile for the remainder of the wall for impact.

Skirt tiles are ideal for a powder room that doesn't need to be fully waterproofed for a shower. Think about doing a contrasting tile around the edge of the room to the floor tile for a bit of fun. If you are using a mosaic tile and you're not tiling your walls, you'll need to do a skirt tile as the edges won't look finished against the wall. Alternatively you could install a proper timber skirting board around the room, too.

CHOOSING GROUT COLOUR

Another important decision! How do you decide which grout colour to opt for? Ask your tiler to mix up a few colour options before you commit so you can see it on a sample tile first. There are no real rules when it comes to picking grout. You may want it to be a feature to make a plain tile stand out more. Alternatively, you might want it to blend in so that the tiles can do the talking.

Choosing metals

Choosing metals for your tapware is a big decision! It's like committing to silver or gold jewellery.

Usually door hardware and taps would match but that's not always possible, especially if you're using a unique tap metal such as an organic weathered brass that tarnishes and changes its colour over time.

When you mix metals, keep the undertone the same. Avoid brass door handles, which are warm, combined with chrome taps, which are in cool-toned colours. Black taps and nickel door handles work much better together.

Tapware colour options have evolved significantly over the past few years. Once there was only chrome, whereas now there are plenty of options.

- Gunmetal
- Bronze
- Chrome
- Copper
- Brass
- Black
- Nickel
- White

Chrome is the most cost-effective option, followed by nickel and black. Speciality metals, such as bronze or antiqued brass, can be more expensive but do give a more luxurious look. Your choice may come down to budget.

Choosing a bath

You'll be tossing up between a back-to-wall bath, built-in bath or free-standing bath. Each has its own pros and cons that you should consider before committing. A free-standing bath looks great but can be a pain to clean around and is not an ideal bath solution if you have to have a bath/shower in one. A built-in bath has a solid, seamless look and also gives you a shelf that runs the entire length of the bath that you can use for sitting on and bathing the kids or resting a glass of wine when soaking yourself! A back-to-wall bath (also referred to as a D-shaped bath because looking at it top down it's shaped a bit like a D) is a great option. It gives you the look of a free-standing bath but without the difficulty of cleaning the back, as it has a curved front but flat back that sits against the wall.

Choosing storage

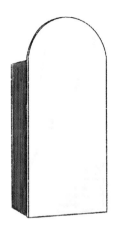

Bathroom storage usually comes at a premium because you're already asking so much in terms of the placement of other important elements from shower heads to toilets to vanity sinks.

The most obvious places for storage in a bathroom are shaving cabinets behind the wall-mounted mirror for important items such as toothbrushes, face creams, first aid items, razors and make-up. Consider installing a powerpoint inside your shaving cabinet to charge your electric toothbrush and razors without having them on the bench.

You could also consider vanity storage for larger items such as hair dryers, hair curlers and straighteners, bathroom cleaning supplies, extra toilet paper rolls and more.

A floor-standing vanity will give you a lot more practical storage space than a wall-mounted vanity.

Choosing a sink

For years now there has been a trend to mount your bathroom sink bowl on top of the vanity bench, making the sink much more of a focal point. While this looks quite striking, it's not always the most practical solution. By mounting your sink underneath the benchtop, you can clean the surface of the bench much more easily by wiping a cloth over the sink. An above-mounted sink gathers more soapy water and is more prone to mould as water pools around the silicone edging.

TAP MOUNTING

Accessibility plays a huge part in bathroom design and the placement of your taps is particularly important. Always consider the length of spout to the basin and the height of the mirror you're hanging above the vanity sink. If you have a long mirror you may find that you do not have enough space to mount a tap on the wall underneath.

If your tap has a curved gooseneck style to it, your mirror may hit the top of the tap when you open it. Play around with all of these elements before committing to any purchases, otherwise on plumbing fit-off day you'll find yourself having to make last minute and expensive adjustments to fix the solution.

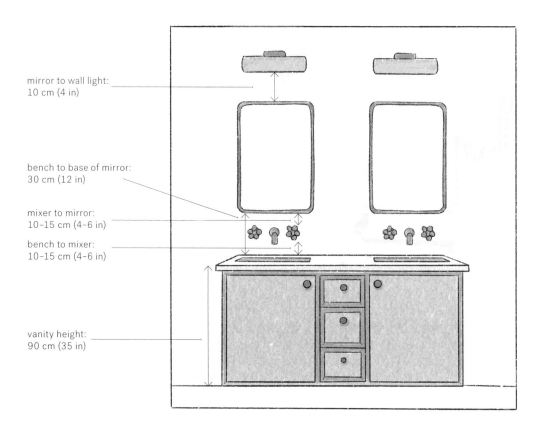

mirror to wall light:
10 cm (4 in)

bench to base of mirror:
30 cm (12 in)

mixer to mirror:
10-15 cm (4-6 in)

bench to mixer:
10-15 cm (4-6 in)

vanity height:
90 cm (35 in)

Lighting

Often there are no windows in a bathroom so lighting is important, especially when doing your make-up or tweezing your eyebrows. Lighting the room from above is usually not enough, even if you opt for a ceiling-mounted light with multiple bulbs. You'll need to add face-height lighting, such as two wall sconces either side of the mirror, for extra lighting at the right height when doing your make-up or checking your reflection before heading out for the day.

Backlighting your mirror is a great way to help light a dark space. There are many brands that now offer backlit mirrors with cool white or warm white colour options and brightness dimmers so you have full control over the light level.

Other ways to brighten a dark bathroom is to use glass and mirrors so you're not blocking any light from other areas of the room. Glass shower screens and partitions instead of tiled shower nooks means light filters through the glass. Mirrors bounce plenty of light around a room so go as large as you can with your above-vanity mounted mirror. And, of course, white tiles are your best friends when it comes to making a bathroom feel brighter. Opt for a cool white rather than a warm white for extra oomph!

next to mirror:
150–160 cm (59–63 in)

above mirror: approximately
10–15 cm (4–6 in)

light above vanity should be about three-quarters of the width of the mirror below it for scale.

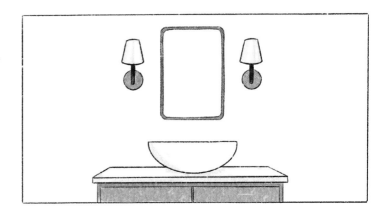

Placing an ensuite

Bathrooms directly next to the bed means there's very little privacy for those who share a bedroom. There was a trend for quite some time to have an ensuite built into a master bedroom without many walls so that it appeared really light and open and airy. But that's the fastest way to kill off the romance in any relationship.

Install a door on the walkway into your ensuite or consider placing your walk-in robe between the bedroom and the ensuite. Putting the toilet in its own room within the ensuite ensures even more privacy. This is particularly important for couples who may wake at different times each morning and want to use the bathroom without waking their partner.

Adding technology

There are so many clever ways to incorporate technology into bathrooms these days; from heated floors and towel rails to speakers integrated into the ceiling. Some bathroom vanities even come with wireless phone-charging stations built into the benchtop.

Placing the toilet-roll holder

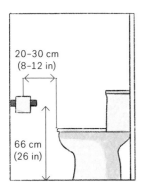

20–30 cm
(8–12 in)

66 cm
(26 in)

Everyone has experienced an awkwardly placed toilet roll, whether it was in a hotel, at a friend's house, or even in their own home. There's always an intuitive spot to hang your toilet-roll holder, but sometimes other elements in the bathroom get in the way of being able to hang it in the ideal place. You don't want to be reaching around behind you and putting your back out each time you need access. Use this guide to help determine the ideal height placement.

Fittings list

If you're not sure what to shop for when it comes to your bathroom shopping list, here's a helpful list of items you can pick and choose from so that you don't miss anything important.

☐ Wall tiles

☐ Floor tiles

☐ Grout

☐ Toilet
(wall mounted will need a flush plate)

☐ Bath

☐ Vanity

☐ Vanity tap

☐ Sink

☐ Shower rose and arm

☐ Shower hose

☐ Shower mixer

☐ Bath mixer
(or switch mixer)

☐ Mirror

☐ Toilet-roll holder

☐ Hand-towel holder

☐ Robe hooks

☐ Towel rack/holder

☐ Shower shelf

☐ Shower screen
and clips

☐ Shower strip drain

☐ Tile grate

☐ Exhaust fan

☐ Light switches and
powerpoint plates

☐ Lighting

☐ Door stop

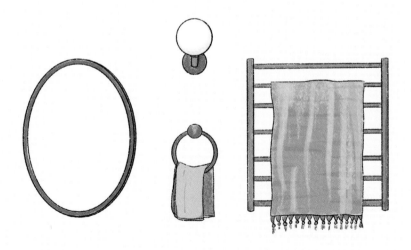

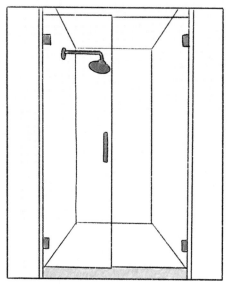

SHOWER SPACE:
90 X 90 CM (35 X 35 IN)

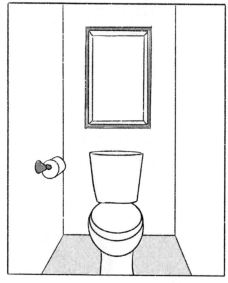

TOILET ROLL MOUNTED AT 65–75 CM
FROM THE FLOOR (26–30 IN)

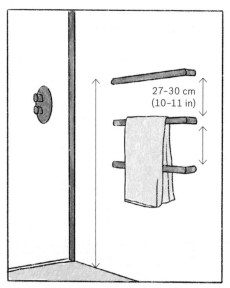

27–30 cm
(10–11 in)

TOWEL RAILS MOUNTED AT 120–160 CM
FROM THE FLOOR (47–62 IN)

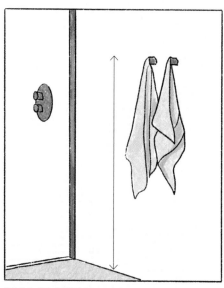

ROBE HOOKS MOUNTED AT 170–180 CM
FROM THE FLOOR (66–70 IN)

Floor plans

Your bathroom is one of the most functional and practical spaces in the house and while you want it to also be beautiful, if the placement of your toilet, shower or bath isn't suitable the whole bathroom becomes a functional mess. The following illustrations will help guide the placement of all of your required services.

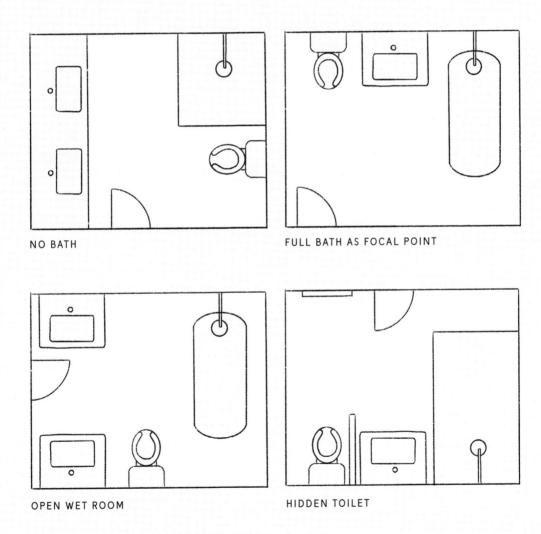

NO BATH

FULL BATH AS FOCAL POINT

OPEN WET ROOM

HIDDEN TOILET

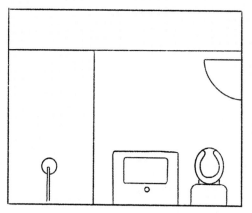

NARROW BATHROOM (GALLEY STYLE)

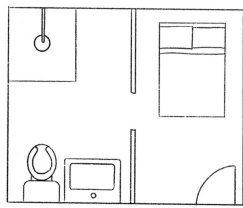

ENSUITE

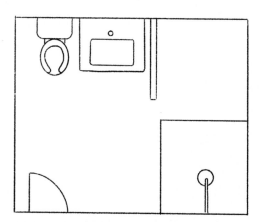

NIB WALL SEPARATING VANITY,
TOILET & SHOWER

Style Your Home

Window treatments

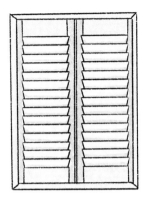

PLANTATION SHUTTERS: These are a great option for controlling light and privacy in the bathroom, but you need to consider the timber-look options rather than timber plantation shutters because of their longevity in wet rooms.

ROLLER BLINDS: Opt for a hard-wearing fabric or even one that is water-resistant, which usually has a high percentage of polyester in it.

PRIVACY FILM: This is a great option if you don't want to block too much light but need privacy.

ACKNOWLEDGEMENTS

People often ask me if writing a book is hard. It's a very different process from a decorating or design project (for obvious reasons) but hard isn't really a word I use to describe writing. When you're passionate about the topic you're writing about and disciplined about your time, the words just keep appearing on the page – as evidenced by the fact that this is the third time I've done this.

I am forever grateful to our clients (past, present and future) who trust us to transform their homes from ugly ducklings to beautiful swans. As someone who didn't go down the path of formal training in the design industry, it never fails to amaze me that I've been incredibly lucky to carve out a career in an industry I hold in awe, knowing that there are so many people out there who would kill to be able to work on some of the projects we work on.

To the team at Hardie Grant, this is the third time we've worked together and the overall dedication to producing incredible books has never changed. Thank you to Alice Hardie-Grant, Lauren Carta, Brigid James, and Emily O'Neill for your beautiful illustrations.

To the incredible team at Emma Blomfield Studio, thank you for all that you do for the business (and me!) daily. Your dedication to the industry, to our clients and to the quality of our projects is what keeps clients coming back to us year after year. And to Justine, thank you for helping me create a strict book-writing schedule and ensuring that I actually stuck to it!

A huge thank you to a number of my close friends who kept on texting me specific questions throughout their own home renovations that helped spark the idea for this book, in particular Emma Taylor. I love that you would disguise most of your texts requesting help for your own home with 'I have an idea for your book …'. Many of your 'ideas' have actually weaved their way into *Style Your Home*.

Mum and Dad, I've thanked you twice before but just in case you hadn't realised, I'm so grateful to you both for giving the three of us kids such incredible childhood memories in our family home. I wouldn't be half the designer I am today if it wasn't for learning from you two all about what home means from such a young age.

To Luke and Alex, while your first few homes were the opposite of what I spend my days crafting, I'm glad to see after all these years you're both now starting to actually 'get' interior design. Maybe your big sister has actually taught you something (or maybe Caitlin and Nicky have threatened to leave you if you didn't start caring about your homes!).

To Dozzie, we shared a home throughout COVID lockdowns and I thought there was a chance I'd kill my best friend after being locked up with you for so long. But it actually provided us with so many fun experiences I'll remember forever. You may not call yourself a stylist or decorator but I was always learning from you as you'd spend hours fussing and obsessing over your bedroom or our shared living space decor. You really do have a knack for styling.

And to Louis, thanks for keeping my lap warm each week while I was writing this book. I know you can't read this but you help make my house a home.

Published in 2025 by Hardie Grant Books, an imprint of Hardie Grant Publishing

Hardie Grant Books (Melbourne)
Wurundjeri Country
Level 11, 36 Wellington Street
Collingwood, Victoria 3066

Hardie Grant North America
2912 Telegraph Ave
Berkeley, California 94705

hardiegrant.com/books

Hardie Grant acknowledges the Traditional Owners of the Country on which
we work, the Wurundjeri People of the Kulin Nation and the Gadigal People
of the Eora Nation, and recognises their continuing connection to the land,
waters and culture. We pay our respects to their Elders past and present.

A catalogue record for this
book is available from the
National Library of Australia

Style Your Home
ISBN 978 1 76145 031 0
ISBN 978 1 76144 341 1 (ebook)

10 9 8 7 6 5 4 3 2 1

Publisher: Alice Hardie-Grant
Head of Editorial: Jasmin Chua
Project Editor: Lauren Carta
Editor: Brigid James
Creative Director: Kristin Thomas
Designer and Illustrator: Emily O'Neill
Head of Production: Todd Rechner
Production Controller: Jessica Harvie

Colour reproduction by Splitting Image Colour Studio
Printed in China by Leo Paper Products LTD

The paper this book is printed on is from FSC®-certified forests and
other sources. FSC® promotes environmentally responsible, socially
beneficial and economically viable management of the world's forests.